Mwakenya:
Real or Phantom?

A Journalist's Harrowing
Experience in the Moi Regime

Jimmy Achira

Nsemia

First Edition December 2010; revised February 2012

Published by: Nsemia Inc. Publishers (www.nsemia.com); Oakville, Ontario, Canada

Edited by Anderea Morara

Cover illustration by Abel Murumba
Layout Design by Truphena K. Matunda
Cover Design and Danielle Pitt

Note for Librarians:
A cataloguing record for this book is available From Library and Archives Canada.

ISBN: 978-1-926906-02-7 Paperback

Lest we forget

for

"Those who don't know history are destined to repeat it."
- *Edmund Burke (1729-1797)*

DEDICATION

This work is dedicated to my parents, grandparents, wife, and children.

To my parents, the late Mzee Joseph Achira Mandere and Mama Salome Nyanchoka Obanyi: through your wisdom and example you cared and brought me up well; sent me to school and taught me to accept responsibility at all times both in difficulty and happiness. For my late father may your soul rest in peace; I treasure you.

To my beloved wife, Margaret Nyakerario Marucha: thank you for all the support you have accorded me.

To my Children – Wycliffe Orutwa, Douglas Nyaporo, Thomas Atunga and Marysalome Mokeira: thank you for your patience in all ways, more so in the final touches of completing this book. I dedicated some of my time and resources at your expense. Each of you brought something fresh and new to the table of life. The last born-Marysalome would question and was ever inquisitive why I would write and tear papers while the rest would marvel and say a word or so of encouragement.

To both paternal and maternal grandparents: you brought up both my parents well and taught them the value of well-behaved children, a factor which was bestowed on me by my parents through the Grace of God.

TABLE OF CONTENTS

ACKNOWLEDGEMENTS

I express my sincere appreciation and gratitude to all who helped me to complete writing this book. The book is a culmination of more than 20 years of soul-searching after my incarceration at Kamiti Maximum Security Prison, Nairobi following the crackdown of the allegedly unlawful underground movement –- Mwakenya in the 1980s.

The main debt in a book of this kind cannot be exhaustively attributed since it is to the many survivors/victims of the infamous Nyayo House torture chambers, dungeons and cells, whose work has been drawn on and referred to.

In writing these words, I am reminded of the loss to the community of writers (journalists) due to the untimely death in 2003 of writer/playwright Wahome Mutahi, whose work was a particular source of inspiration towards writing of this book.

Equally, I am reminded of the passing on of the political icon, and a vibrant Parliamentarian George Moseti Anyona in 2003, who was my mentor and model in the world of politics – may God rest his soul in eternal peace.

I am indebted to the Citizens for Justice (CFJ) and the People Against Torture (PAT) from whom some ideas and ways of presentation of this story were first worked out. The the idea of chronologizing my story first came into my mind six months into my time at Kamiti Maximum Security Prison/ detention camp.

I am thankful to many friends and colleagues in different parts of the world for their stimulating thoughts and encouragement. Specifically, I am indebted to my editors Prof. Peter Kareithi and the late Bob Hitchcock both of who I worked with the Nation Newspapers Limited as a cub reporter between May 1982 and 1984.

The final preparation of the manuscript was greatly helped by the fast and efficient secretarial support of Joshua Wafula and Shadrack Ngetich of Shaddy Enterprise of Nakuru, Kenya. They patiently deciphered my handwriting to type out the manuscript. I am very grateful to their patience and good work.

Equally, I am deeply indebted to the Rt. Rev. Bishop T. C. Mugendi of the larger Catholic Diocese of Kisii (DOK) for standing by me during my trials, the tribulations and thereafter the incarceration in 1988. May God rest his soul in eternal peace.

I am grateful to Charles Obanyi Achira of New Jersey (USA) and Josephine Kemunto-Onwong'a of Baltimore, Maryland, (USA) for the necessary support and well-judged pressure to fulfill the mission of writing this book.

My thanks go to Dr. C. F. Onyango of Centre for Multiparty Democracy (CMD), lawyers Gershom Otachi Bw'Omanwa and Ken Ogetto both of ICTR, Arusha, Tanzania for their enthusiasm and encouragement, which was a great source of inspiration to me.

I wish to express my sincere thanks to journalists George Obanyi and Joseph Nyanoti for their positive criticism and support in improving the clarity of my language.

I will not forget to offer my special thanks to Evans Nyakang'o of Kenya Revenue Authority, Nairobi and Francis Mwarucha of Teachers Service Commission, Nairobi for their unreserved support, which often lifted my spirit when the going got tough during the final touches of this book. Equally, I am indebted to Moraa Gitaa for devoting her energy and time in editing and proof-reading the entire manuscript.

Every author is indebted to all those who have influenced their lives. I can never be grateful enough for all those men and women whom God brought across my path over the years, the way he used them to enrich me and add to my understanding of the world affairs, particularly Africa's socio-political set-up.

Tolerance and encouragement from my family (especially my wife, children and parents) has been another indispensable ingredient to finishing this book. I am particularly thankful to my beloved wife lady Margaret Nyakerario, who over the years has been my closest friend and advisor; whose insights have greatly contributed to my journalism career and the writing this book.

Importantly, I am immensely grateful to my brothers and sisters. You are all special in one way or the other. However, I am obliged to single out my brother, lawyer David Onyancha, for his most sincere legal advice, moral and unlimited financial support directed either to me directly or my family, while I was out of the country for my journalism studies or absent from my family for one reason or the other.

I am also indebted to those who helped in the preparation of this book for publication. I owe special thanks to my longtime associate, Dr. Isaac Maragia, whose editorial skills and research enabled me to select and recast materials from various sources into a suitable form for this kind of book.

Inevitably, a book of this nature cannot be written without immense help from others, I would like to thank the many Nyayo House torture victims/survivors, who opened doors and actively assisted the work of research towards completion of this book.

Any inaccuracies or distortions which occur herein are to be entirely ascribed to the author, and not to those without whose help the writing of this book could have been difficult and incomplete.

Finally, yet importantly, those whose names have not been mentioned here is because of space. They should not interpret it to mean that their contributions in any form towards the completion of this book were insignificant. There are many whose support and prayers were critical to the success of this book. May God bless you all.

Jimmy Achira

June 2010, Nakuru- Kenya

FOREWORD

Every book has a history. Most times it is not worth recounting. In this case, I believe it is. *"Mwakenya: Real or Phantom? A Journalist's Harrowing Experience"* needs recounting.

After consultations with the author and going through the manuscript, the book needs serious recounting and readers need to be told the historical background which led to the arrest of the author and being 'processed' through the torture chambers of Nyayo House to Kamiti Maximum Security Prison.

I believe it is worth knowing the circumstances under which this book is based.

"The ascendancy to the Presidency in August 1978 and the period immediately after proved President Daniel Arap Moi, a man who loved his country and was willing to listen and work hard to develop it. It also showed that Moi had little regard for the script of classical democracy. It was during this period that the system of electing party officials – the ruling party then Kenya African National Union (KANU) and in some cases MPs, on the basis of official lists prepared by power-brokers, was invented"[1]

It was a system that persisted all through Moi-KANU era and was responsible for the death of internal democracy in KANU and was especially debilitating when the party was the only means of political mobility both for individuals and ideas.

However, it was after 1982 that the Moi we came to know clearly emerged from the formative cocoon of fighting the coup and dismantling the alternative power bases of

---

1 (Mutuma Mathiu) Revise Editor with *Daily Nation* then in 2002, wrote in an article "Inventing Bad Alternatives To Democracy And Liberty" published in a Special Supplement of December 24, 2002 titled: "Moi: End of an Era"

such rivals as Mr. Charles Mugane Njonjo. At the KANU elections he pretty much hand-picked the officials and the country was finally in his fist; he was the undisputed leader -- no serious opposition within the borders, other than the clergy and a few eccentric Members of Parliament (MPs).

KANU was under his thumb, so was the provincial administration and the judiciary. From that point on, the direction that the country was to take purely depended on his (Moi's) whims and his assumed democratic instincts.

Sadly, it was after the 1982 coup attempt that the retired President Moi emerged in his darkest colours. It was during this period that Moi directed the most sustained assault on the last vestiges of democracy.

In August 1986, the KANU National Delegates Conference scrapped the secret ballot voting system and replaced it with 'Queue Voting', seriously undermining elections as a process of delegating the authority of the people`s representatives.

Towards the end of 1986, a Bill to amend the constitution was moved in parliament to remove the security of Tenure of Constitutional offices such as that of the Controller and Auditor-General.

In August 1988, a similar Bill was taken to the House (Parliament) and passed; this time targeting judges of the High Court and the Court of Appeal.

This period too was a time of horror in the history of Human Rights in Kenya. Already in early 1986, a crackdown on those Kenyans perceived to be with dissenting views about the government had been put in motion.

Under the guise of rooting out subversives, particularly referred to as "Mwakenya" (*Muungano wa Wakenya*) the police unleashed such a reign of terror that a wide cross-section of people's lives were destroyed.

In December 1986, the author was among those branded as being members of the unlawful society – Mwakenya, and was arrested (picked up) in Kisii town and driven to Nairobi after two days stay at Kisii Police Divisional Headquarters, under the watch and guard of the then dreaded Special Branch, a unit of the Kenya Police. The author ended up in Nyayo House torture chambers for forty-five days.

Freedom of thought and expression were particularly hated and many journalists and academics were processed through the Nyayo House torture chambers to prisons and detention camps in Kenya.

Dissent was dealt with through arrests, police searches and harassment, torture and often detention without trial. KANU had created an invasive and oppressive police state in Kenya. And the retired president had been given a carte blanche -- according to his wishes to meddle in every institution of government.

Moi had also arrogated himself the right, more than ever before, to determine what people could and could not think, could not achieve. Blind loyalty was the only currency; and often even that was not enough.

By 1988, the wanton abuse of power had built up the pressure that was to finally destroy the one party state. But it was the election of that year (February 1988) that was the final push.

The queue-voting method was a complete mess. Described by the then Bishop of Nakuru Catholic Diocese Rt. Rev. Ndingi Mwana Nzeki as totalitarian, it was a season of madness during which KANU and the retired President Moi completely destroyed democratic reason.

In January 1987, the author found himself being led to prison. This was about nine years after Moi took over leadership of Kenya from the founding father of the Nation - the late Mzee Jomo Kenyatta, who passed on in his sleep at Mombasa State House on August 22, 1978.

In prison, the author joined the hundreds or so others who had been imprisoned/detained on charges ranging from possession of seditious literature to taking of an illegal oath.

Like others, Jimmy Achira, had been taken to court after official working hours and without legal representation. As many others who had been jailed for those offences, he had been tortured into admitting the charges and was convicted and sentenced to two years in jail.

The fore-going, illustrates the two faces of the Moi government's human rights record. The man, who had ushered in his regime with what looked like intentions to correct his predecessor's bad human rights record, later turned his guns against the same rights.

The turnabout was a result of events that suddenly engulfed retired president Moi and which, though not able to rationalize his acts, at least explains them.

What primarily worsened the political situation in Kenya was the attempted coup of August 1, 1982. The coup so shocked and annoyed Moi, that from then on he never offered any apologies for his government's abuse of human rights.

After the coup was crushed, some 2,000 Kenya Air Force (K.A.F) personnel and at least 1,000 plus civilians were detained. Riots and protests raged all over the city of Nairobi as the crackdown on the coup attempt supporters intensified.

Moi then proceeded to influence Parliament to change the constitution and turn Kenya into a de'Jure single party state and to legitimize the flooding of prisons and detention camps with political prisoners!

By March 1986, President Moi's government had detained and jailed numerous Kenyans under the provisions of the Public Security Act. The majority were mainly accused of belonging to an underground movement called Mwakenya, which was accused of trying to topple the government using unlawful means.

The trials of Mwakenya suspects had the dubious distinction of being held late in the evening when there were no family members and lawyers in the courts, which were largely filled by plain-clothes police officers comprising of Special Branch and Criminal Investigation Police Units.

It was also a means to cover up the torture that the suspects had undergone while in detention. And hence, not surprisingly almost all of them (suspects) 'pleaded guilty' to the charges, once they were brought to court.

The crackdown continued throughout 1986 up to almost the end of 1987. It spilled over to early 1988. Journalist Achira was a victim when the crackdown climaxed towards the end of 1986.

In fact, retired President Moi was quoted in July 1987 saying that the suspects were tortured only to get information from them. He (Moi) loudly wondered how else they (government officials) could get the information they needed except through torture!

The Mwakenya crackdown saw the jailing and exiling of academics and students from the University of Nairobi, where many lecturers were accused of teaching Marxism. On the other hand, those who toed the party line and the so-called Moi-KANU policies were promoted and had their salaries raised. This action, in fact seriously stifled the rights of students and of academic freedom.

The crackdown continued and gloom was all over the country, as Moi and the KANU government assumed an arrogance of great magnitude.

To them, the opposition had been exposed and forever destroyed. The years between 1986 and 1988 became better known as "the years Kenyans had to look behind their backs and shoulders before they spoke anything perceived to be anti-government", for fear of the then dreaded Special Branch Police.

But Kenyans who were 'thirsty for change', had to pay a heavy price for it; as the ruling class that opposed the re-introduction of multiparty politics and predicted that the country could degenerate into chaos because of the many political parties held to their guns.

This became true when politically instigated clashes wrongly called "tribal clashes" broke out in parts of Rift Valley, Coast and Nyanza Provinces.

This was the most serious human rights violation to occur during the 24 years of the Moi-KANU regime. Hundreds of people were killed; others displaced from "their homes", pregnant mothers had their wombs ripped open and women were openly raped.

The Kenyan justice system, as noted in the case of Mwakenya trials, played a willing ally in the violation of human rights. Trumped-up charges were frequently made in complicity with the judiciary, arising from undue government pressure and interference.

The failed coup attempt of August 1, 1982 is widely regarded as the turning point in Moi's relationship with the Kenyan public. Until then, Moi drew his Security from the perception that he was a popular leader. After the coup; Moi initiated a purge to rid the country of any perceived threats. As part of this increasing paranoia, Moi sought to control as many aspects of the Kenyans public and even private affairs as possible.

This dark epoch in the history of Kenya, is thus the basis of this book – *"Mwakenya: Real or A Phantom? A Journalist's Harrowing Experience"*.

Dr. Carey Francis Onyango, Ph.D
June, 2010. - Nairobi, Kenya

PROLOGUE

This book is based on my enduring experience as a person who was arrested, bundled into Nyayo House torture chambers, dungeons and cells. I was held incommunicado for 45 days and was subjected to torture sessions at the infamous torture chambers under the stewardship of one James Opiyo of the defunct Special Branch Police Unit; on the allegation that I was a member of a clandestine movement called Mwakenya.

My harrowing experience was deepened as a political prisoner at both the country's Kamiti Maximum Security prison and Kodiaga main prison (Kisumu), for the two years I was incarcerated.

I was particularly helped in the drafting of this book by the stimuli and insights offered by activities, programmes and participation in seminars, workshops and conferences that had the element(s) of development journalism and human rights aspects. I have also benefited from accessing and reading a lot of literature on human rights.

I have, of course, constantly cross-checked and compared my own experiences with those of my colleagues in all cases where these are reflected in books and above all in specialized publications. Though I have, over my many years of work in the world of journalism, largely forgotten the names of the authors and the titles of their publications (with apologies), my indebtedness to them remains.

For the authors of those publications which served as stimuli, I, at this point therefore, wish to offer them collectively my sincere thanks. Among them Koigi wa Wamwere for his write-up: *The Epilogue*; Journalist Mwenda Njoka's various write-ups about Mwakenya and opening of Nyayo House torture chambers; Scholar Egara Kabaji, Hon. Gitobu Imanyara (publisher and editor of "*The Nairobi Law Monthly*").

This book is based on lifelong experiences starting from my arrest in Kisii Town on December 15, 1986, while on vacation from St. Augustine University of Tanzania (SAUT); successor to Nyegezi Social Training Institute's School of Journalism based at the Lake Town of Mwanza, Tanzania.

My world view has, of course, been influenced by the experience and exposure I have had with the mainstream media, while working as a cub reporter, senior reporter and later on in middle management editorial positions. My perspectives have also been enriched by exposure to and interaction with politicians within and outside Kenya, fellow journalists and people from the Diaspora in the arenas of communication, development and various facets of socio-economic and religious life. All these sources of stimuli have contributed to my motivation to document this repressive chapter of Kenya's history.

Specifically, the late acknowledged journalist and actor, Wahome Mutahi, inspired me in the course of our sharing to embark on the abandoned manuscript and by end of 2003 it was completed only awaiting compilation, editing and proof reading. By end of May 2009 I was satisfied that a documentation of my arrest, torture, incarceration and anguish, was then ready for public 'consumption'.

Looking back to my over 20 years of work in the world of journalism and mass communication and the political dynamics of the country, I have no regrets for having been incarcerated. To my parents, wife, children and those relatives who supported me in one way or the other during this trying period, I am eternally grateful.

My story was given credence by the opening of the infamous Nyayo House torture chambers, on February 11, 2003, although I had already been motivated to complete the manuscript after the 24-year old Moi-KANU regime had been swept out of power by the defunct National Rainbow Coalition (NARC) on December 27, 2002 during Kenya's third Multiparty General Elections.

The book, which is segmented into eleven chapters, is divided into two parts – Part One, which consists of chapters one – four, discusses the arrest of the author, his detention at Kisii and Kileleshwa police stations in Kisii and Nairobi respectively, 45 days of torture sessions at Nyayo House torture chambers and why jail was a *Better Option.*

Part Two of the book covers chapters five to eleven. It deals mainly with the opening of Nyayo House torture chambers on February 11, 2003. Before chapter five, scholar Egara Kabaji examines *the "Torture Chambers of Crime and Punishment".*

Amnesty International (AI) says torture victims should be accorded justice, for there is no immunity for torturers. At the same time AI explains 'What is Torture?' and 'What are Crimes of Torture under International Law?'

The questions about the Moi–KANU government's justification for torture and one being held 'incommunicado' still linger...

Lastly the author asks: After opening of the Nyayo House torture chambers, what next? Were torture chambers an afterthought?

Jimmy Achira,
Nakuru, Kenya;
June 2010

QUOTABLE QUOTES

"History shows that dictatorships in their last days target thuggery to democratic reformers in desperate attempts to cling to power. The **Shah** *of Iran had his* **Savak, Papa Doc** *of Haiti had his* **Tom-toms macoute** *and Ceausescu of Romania had his Securitate. No amount of intimidation, threats or even political murders can stop the march towards democratization in Kenya any longer."-Raila Odinga, quoted in Society Magazine, October, 1999*

"When dictatorship does not change; it must be torture. As for who was responsible, torture in Kenya was a scorpion. Its head was the president. It stung with the police to protect the head. In between, the head and the tail there were prosecutors, judges so the police did not torture people for and on their own behalf. Politicians ordered torture to protect their own power and wealth."
- Koigi Wa Wamwere, Ex-detainee

It was on July 5th, 1990 that I was sent to the bowels of hell in the basement of Nairobi's Nyayo House Torture Chambers. This happened at 11:00am. I was stripped naked and then thrown in a water logged cell and remained there until mid-night when I was served with detention papers"
John Khaminwa, Human Rights Lawyer & Ex-detainee.

"Kenyans today enjoy many freedoms that came through the sacrifice of a few that dared dissent against former President Moi's dictatorial regime. In the paranoia of the day, Moi's elaborate web of security netted many

that posed little or no threat to the regime. Yet these victims encountered unnecessary inhuman torture, detention and jail."

- Dr. Matunda Nyanchama, ICT Professional & Publisher

"It is instructive that after the abortive 1982 coup, President Daniel Moi, had fallen back on intelligence briefings – exclusive only to the Head of State – as one of intelligence greatest strengths. He used intelligence briefings to understand and dismantle the networks of those who were perceived as anti-establishment and, by extension, at least in the President's view, a threat to national stability.

"The National Security Intelligence Service (N.S.I.S) had previously been known as the Special Branch. Then they were a police unit with powers to arrest and detain.

"The Special Branch's dreaded officers would hunt down political dissidents and those who lived to tell the tale have told frightening stories of torture and harassment.

"They kept tabs on everyone and tapped phones to ensure that those who served the Moi government were loyal and could be trusted never to reveal any government secrets that would benefit opponents of the system. Anybody who defied the system was simply hunted down and his political machinery -- real or imagined, systematically dismantled."

"Sunday Nation", December 3, 2006

"Many in their 20s and 30s now, Mwakenya story reads like a fairy tale as they grew up knowing retired President Moi as a comical and nice old man. Kenyans, in their otherwise spirit of resilience and 'moving on' with life and addressing the current 'ills' all too easily forget or gloss over serious historical human rights abuses."

Otachi Bw'Omanwa, Defence Attorney at ICTR, Arusha, Tanzania

"It was on July 5, 1990 that I was sent to the bowels of hell in the basement of Nairobi's Nyayo House torture chambers. This happened at 11:00am. I was stripped naked and then thrown in a water logged cell and remained there until mid-night when I was served with detention papers"

John Khaminwa, Human Rights Lawyer & Ex-detainee

"Moi was a man who achieved greatness by patiently and loyally toiling for the great Jomo Kenyatta, even while being humiliated by State House courtiers until the grace of Charles Njonjo, the then Attorney General's legal instruments of the State favoured his (Moi's) succession to Kenyatta's coveted throne. He occupied for 24 years with an iron fist of an accomplished dictator, even sending his mentor (Njonjo) to political limbo with the disgrace of being a traitor to Nyayoism."

Prof. Anyang' Nyong'o, Legislator & political crusader

"The James Opiyo squad of Special Branch police officers based at Nyayo House Police Station were sadistic beasts and their leader (Opiyo) was the devil incarnate."

Anonymous Mwakenya Victim, USA

"In all places where dictatorial regimes have collapsed, from Romania to former Yugoslavia to Argentina and Chile, living dictators are being asked to account for the errors of their regimes. So should we in Kenya"

Prof. Peter Wanyande, University of Nairobi's political scientist quoted in the Sunday Nation, February 16, 2003.

INTRODUCTION

I was arrested in Kisii Town on December 15, 1986 at about 5:15pm and was booked at the Kisii Divisional Police Cells of Kisii District of Nyanza Province, Western Kenya for two days.

On December 17, 1986 I moved to Nairobi through Nyayo House 24th floor and sent to Kileleshwa Police Station where I was booked until about 7.45 pm of same day (December 17, 1986) before I was blindfolded and driven for about three hours through various roads, streets and avenues of Nairobi before I ended up at Nyayo House torture chambers.

At the torture chambers, I was tortured, harassed and later on – after 45 days taken to Nairobi Law Courts hurriedly, where I was convicted and sentenced (jailed) for two years for allegedly being a member of Mwakenya, purportedly an underground movement according to the then Moi government.

Today (after opening of Nyayo House torture chambers) about seven years ago, I hereby give an account of what transpired at the Nyayo House torture chambers.

I was a victim of torture at Nyayo House basement cells and torture chambers, on the 24th, 25th and 26th floors of the towering Nyayo House building which accommodates Nairobi Provincial Administration Offices, and the Ministry of Immigration offices, among other government facilities.

The torture chambers are a replica of the death chambers. First, I wish to thank God for having cared for me all the days I was at the Nyayo House torture chambers, dungeons and cells, especially the days I underwent the torture sessions at both the torture chambers and the dungeons at the basement, which were opened to the public by the defunct National Rainbow Coalition (NARC) Administration on February 11, 2003.

What on earth are these torture chambers/dungeons and cells there for? It is all in this book. *"If you have read accounts of Ugandan Dictator Idi Amin's Secret Research Bureau (SRB) or the Securitate of Nicolae Ceausescu, former Romanian strongman, then you can picture how the Nyayo House Squad operated. Do these Kenyan men (torturers) know what happened to the SRB or Securitate Agents when their masters fell?"* (*Society Magazine of October, 1999 Issue No 26*).

This is an epic story filled with fear and tears. Therefore, it is a book that demands to be read at a sitting.

Jimmy Achira
June 2010 Nakuru, Kenya

PART ONE

Achira being led to underground cells at Nairobi Law Courts after conviction and sentence on January 29th 1987.

MOI CHANGED TACT
AFTER AUGUST 1, 1982

An enduring mystery in Kenya's history is how junior officers of the Kenya Air Force (KAF) planned a rebellion and executed the failed takeover of President Daniel Arap Moi's government on August 1, 1982. It is inconceivable that the soldiers made their move despite the touted intelligence network headed by the dreaded post-independence spy, the late James Kanyotu.

It is a matter of speculation as to what exactly transpired a few days prior to the coup attempt; what is in no doubt is that President Moi significantly changed tact after the event. The failed coup turned him into a dictator and heralded crackdowns over the next few years on all forms of "dissent".

Kanyotu's[1] intelligence network was central to the arrests, detentions, tortures, and disappearances that marked the dark years. Yet looked in hindsight, the coup was not an event out of the blue; it was part of a process in the struggle for change.

Not long before the attempted coup, Moi's Government had amended the infamous Section 2A of the Constitution to make Kenya a Single-Party State.

Detention without trial had also made a comeback as Kanyotu's intelligence network pursued radical university lecturers, constitutional and human rights lawyers who dared to defend so-called dissident journalists, political scientists, university student leaders and budding political activists.

---

1 Kanyotu was the Head of the police Special Branch, the security wing that was responsible for spying on and arresting suspected political dissidents

After the coup attempt of August 1, 1982, it was an open season, other than military plotters who were sentenced to death or lengthy jail terms; other prominent victims included Mr. Raila Odinga, then Deputy Director of Kenya Bureau of Standards (KEBS). Raila was one of the four civilians charged with treason before the charges were withdrawn and substituted with detention without trial. Others were Professor Vincent Otieno of University of Nairobi and Journalist Otieno Mak'Onyango then managing editor, Standard on Sunday. That was not all, President Moi, as if he was not through with the disloyal KAF personnel, turned viciously on presumed disloyal elements in private and public sectors -- universities, institutions of higher learning and civil society.

The author of this book was a victim of the crack-down on alleged disloyal Kenyans with recalcitrant political views, the so-called dissidents.

CHAPTER ONE

Arrest in Kisii Town

It was in the afternoon of December 15, 1986 at about 4:35 p.m. I was with a friend, David Omenge, who is also a home mate – we come from the same village in Bogichora Location, West Mugirango. We were heading for Capital Hotel Bar and Restaurant in the heart of Kisii Town, opposite the then Standard Chartered Bank, where the present National Bank of Kenya, Kisii Branch is located.

The Capital Hotel Bar and Restaurant located on the first floor of a three storey building was one of the popular joints in Kisii Town. Our key objective was to go there and quench the afternoon 'thirst' as we were all in need of something cold. I had suggested to Omenge that we can have an Export (a beer) for that matter at Capital.

After all, Omenge was a good friend and we had not met for some time; as I had been away for almost a year and 11 months at college in Mwanza Tanzania. As we were in the corridor of the first floor of the building, heading for the pub, two Security Intelligence Officers (Special Branch police, as they were known in those days), from the District Security Intelligence Office approached me. One of them (I do well re-call his name – Inspector Kigen) politely requested me to accompany him downstairs, claiming that he had been sent to find out some details about my *harambee*[1] which took place at Kisii Hotel over that weekend.

I quickly told him, *"It is not fair for you to interrupt my program and yet your boss – Supt. Gerald Ndungu, was present at the harambee. He even contributed Kshs 100 during the function."* Insp. Kigen was equally quick to tell

1 Fundraiser

me that it was his boss who wanted to talk to me at the station (Police Divisional Offices).

In fact, the previous weekend – December 13, 1986, I had organized an harambee which was attended by among others, the then MP of Kitutu East (now Kitutu Masaba), and Hon. Abuya Abuya, while Wundanyi MP then Hon. Mashengu wa Mwachofi among others sent his apologies as he was one of the guests.

The chief guest was the then Chief Accountant of the Pyrethrum Board of Kenya (PBOK), Henry Obwocha – who was later to become a Member of Parliament for West Mugirango (1992 – 2007).

The aim of the harambee was to raise funds towards my studies, to assist in supplementing tuition fees and other educational expenses to enable me to complete my Journalism studies at St. Augustine University of Tanzania (SAUT) then known as Nyegezi Social Training Institute (NSTI). I was then a second year student of Journalism, and I was on December 1986 vacation.

In fact, I told Inspector Kigen to allow me to talk to a friend at the pub, and then we would go to see his boss (Supt. Ndungu). He had insisted that I must accompany him to the office, where his boss was waiting. At the pub, I bought myself and my friend, Omenge, a drink -- four exports and we got settled talking at the counter of the pub as Insp. Kigen and his team waited patiently. Those days Export beer was usually bought in sets of two by whoever was buying. In fact that is why I bought four -- two for myself and two for my friend Omenge!

Inspector Kigen was patient for about 30 minutes, waiting in a Land Rover parked outside the pub, whereas his 'boys' -- two of them, who apparently were on the same mission, waited along the corridors of the pub; I was later to be told by friends.

It was approaching 6:25p.m., the two 'boys' (Special

Branch police), who were known to me approached and told me that they had been sent by Inspector Kigen, who was outside the pub. Although it was raining, I obliged and informed my friend Omenge that I had been called by Supt. Ndungu of Special Branch at the Kisii Police Divisional Headquarters.

As I walked downstairs of Capital Hotel and Restaurant in the company of two Special Branch police officers, I saw the grey Land Rover and two other Special Branch officers inside.

Inspector Kigen told me that since it was raining, I was to go with them in the Land Rover, he pointed towards Standard Chartered Bank, where the vehicle was parked. I had no objection. It barely took five minutes to reach the vehicle, a grey Land Rover with registration number KWE 547, which was sandwiched between two other Land Rovers; This in fact, was the official vehicle of District Special Branch police boss (DSBO). I was driven straight to the DSBO's Office. I was seated in front together with Insp. Kigen and the driver – Police Constable Araka. There were two police officers (dressed in civilian attire) seated at the back seats of the Land Rover.

As we disembarked outside the DSBO's Office, I was still not suspicious of anything, until I was received by Supt. Ndungu, who at that time, unlike the other times we had met, was apparently very unfriendly. He lifted the phone and asked for a Mr. Wachira as he introduced himself. After a while he received a telephone call on another line. *"Yes, I am Supt. Gerald Ndungu, DSIO, Kisii and I want to talk to Mr. Wachira who was formerly at Siaya and is now there."* (I learnt later that he was referring to Supt. Wachira who was one of the torture squad members at Nyayo House, Nairobi).

After two or three minutes, as I was still seated in Ndungu's office, he responded to an incoming call: *"Sir I have found Mr. Achira and he is with me here in the office.*

What can I do with him?........... "Yes sir, Yes, Yes sir, Yes sir."

After three yes sirs, Supt. Ndungu turned to me and simply told me. *"Mr. Achira, from now on you are under arrest, and you are wanted in Nairobi. I will therefore, keep you here until those who want you come from Nairobi for you. They will either come tonight or tomorrow."* Supt. Ndungu casually stated.

I simply asked him (Ndungu) why they had arrested me. He said *"Mr. Achira I am under instructions and I know no reason(s) for your arrest. However; you will not be in police cells, I will let you stay at the booking office of the station until those who need you arrive from Nairobi."*

It was now 7:15 p.m. I asked Supt. Ndungu to allow me to go to my residence and take some medicine to my son Douglas Nyaporo, who was then about two years old. He accepted and firmly instructed Inspector Kigen and two other officers plus the driver Araka to drive me to my residence and bring me back to the station before 9:00 p.m.

Indeed, they obliged. After all, although they were Special Branch officers, they were all the same policemen and they had to obey an order from their senior. The officers accompanied me to my residence but we passed through two places – Capital Hotel in Kisii town and then Kisii Hotel. At Capital Hotel, I told my friends, including my home mate David Omenge, and at Kisii Hotel Mr. Samuel Kigadi, that I was under arrest and I was being taken to Nairobi the same night or the following day, quoting Supt. Ndungu.

I remember well to have told the manager to inform the owner of the Hotel, Mzee John Oigara. In fact, Mzee Oigara was my friend and even at the time of writing this book he remained my friend and a good advisor in many areas of life.

The reason for the manager to inform Mzee Oigara about my arrest was to ensure that he (Mzee Oigara) banked the money collected from the Saturday 13 1986 harambee held at his hotel (Kisii Hotel). I had kept the cash at Mzee Oigara's hotel safe after the harambee and I had planned to bank the cash after the weekend. Mzee Oigara, the proprietor of Kisii Hotel Ltd., indeed banked the cash on my behalf at National Bank of Kenya Kisii Branch the following day – December 16, 1986 -- for I had left my Bank Account details with his Manager, Mr. Kigadi.

Before I was taken away from Capital Hotel, two other friends had joined us (I and Omenge). They were James Mugare Njuguna (now deceased) – may God rest his soul in eternal peace. The late Njuguna was then the Licensing Officer with Kenya Broadcasting Corporation (KBC) and Baraza Muricho, who was an Information Officer at Kisii District Information Office and a Kenya News Agency (KNA) reporter. Mr. Muricho was later transferred to Nyandarua District, and lately, as I was finalizing the writing of this book, he was the District Information Officer incharge of Trans Nzoia, Kitale in the North Rift.

At Capital Hotel, nobody suspected that I had been arrested -- not even my friends the late Mugare, Muricho and Omenge, until I came back with three plain-clothes police officers and I informed them of my arrest. It was after that, that the news of my arrest spread in Kisii Town that night like a bush fire. Some reports were that I had been flown to Nairobi, others that I had been taken to Kisumu. I was taken to Nairobi in Supt. Ndungu's company via the Kisii–Kericho–Nakuru highway on December 17, 1986.

I must here point out that it was well known that I was a *"controversial and brave journalist who feared nobody and reported without fear or favour"*. I did carry out investigative journalism and in-depth reporting without malice. In fact, I was appreciated by my employer – *Nation Newspapers Ltd.* and the public at large. Before I went to pursue my journalism studies in Tanzania I was the Kisii-based, Nation Staff Correspondent (retained).

I was in fact posted to Kisii as Nation's Retained Correspondent at the beginning of July 1982, after a stint at *The East African Standard* newspapers as one of its Nairobi-based freelance correspondents. I was at *The Standard* between February 1980 and May 1982.

Interestingly, when I went back to Capital Hotel, the three plain-clothes police officers under the command of Inspector Kigen, stood next to me at the counter of the pub with my friends, as I confided with David Omenge over what had transpired at Supt. Ndungu's Office, and consequently that Supt. Ndungu had informed me that I was under arrest. I told Omenge to get in touch with my family members, more so my elder brother - Mr. Nicholas Abuga Achira, who was then working at Central Bank of Kenya (CBK), Nairobi. I gave Omenge the telephone numbers for my brother for both residence and office.

At this point I bought my friends some drinks and cleared my bill, after which we left and wished them good time until we would meet next. I did not know that my saying goodbye to my friends was going to be the last until after two years and for others until after four years.

At Kisii Hotel, where we (I and the three Special Branch police officers went to meet the manager, Mr. Kigadi, the story was the same. I also wished him (the manager) and friends who were at the hotel then, good times.

Those whom I wished well and said bye to included friends and relatives, who came to see me at the Kisii Police Station the following days on 16th and 17th of December, 1986.

Among them were Messrs Nehemiah Nyakwara (now retired Information Officer), Peter Angwenyi (free-lance sports journalist), my wife Margaret Nyakerario with my son Douglas, who was then one and a half years old, my sister Martha Kwamboka, my cousin Charles Abuga Migosi and a host of other relatives and friends.

Just to refresh my memory, during the six-hour

harambee function at the open place of Kisii Hotel, notable personalities who attended and participated by donating towards my journalism studies at Tanzania's St. Augustine University of Tanzania (SAUT), Mwanza included the then Auditor-General (State Corporations) Mr. Abincha Onono, Mr. Charles Onyancha then of Kimani Accountants and Auditors -- now Orange Democratic Movement (ODM) MP of Bonchari, South Kisii District -- Mr. Samuel Mokaya (then with Montedison Kenya Ltd. as an Operations Manager), Mr. Samuel Nyamato (then Finance and Operations Manager with then Trans-National Finance Company), Nairobi (now Trans-National Bank).

The chief guest was the then Chief Accountant with Pyrethrum Board of Kenya (PBOK), Nakuru, and Mr. Henry Obwocha – who was later to become the MP for West Mugirango for three terms consecutively: 1992-2007.

He was assisted by the then MP for Kitutu East, Hon. Abuya Abuya, who later became a commissioner with Electoral Commission of Kenya (ECK)[2].

By local standards, the function was high profile and it was well covered by the District Security Intelligence Office led by the District Security Intelligence Officer (DSIO) himself Supt. Gerald Ndungu; popularly referred to as District Special Branch Officer (DSBO).

At Kisii Hotel, after I cleared my bills in respect to the Saturday December 13, 1986 function, we then proceeded to my residence at Oyugis Township (now Rachuonyo District). The bills were as a result of the funds-drive party which I hosted, at the hotel over that weekend, where my guests had meals and drinks and there were pending bills which I was to clear the following day – December 14, 1986 -- but I pushed the date to Monday December 15, 1986; the day I was arrested!

---

2 ECK was disbanded late 2008 and replaced with Interim Independent Electoral Commission (IIEC),, which has since been replaced by IEBC.

At My House with Police Officers

We arrived at Oyugis Township – 22 kilometers from Kisii Town through Nyakoe Market Centre; Mosocho, Roga then Oyugis Town in Rachuonyo District.

I was in the company of three plain-clothes police officers from Kisii District Security Intelligence Office. The three officers under the command of Inspector Kigen drove me to Oyugis (my residence then) in the official DSBO Land Rover – KWE 547. On arrival at Oyugis it was 7:45 p.m.

In the house were my wife, Margaret Nyakerario, my two sons – Wyclifee Orutwa, seven years then, Douglas one year and six months, the house help (by the name Juliana) and a Sudanese student friend – Mr. Angelo Lokoyome. Mr. Lokoyome was a Journalism student colleague at St. Augustine University of Tanzania (SAUT), Mwanza, Tanzania; who had accompanied me home for the December holidays. They were all in the sitting room, except my wife and the house help – Juliana, who were in the kitchen – apparently preparing supper for the children and the guest.

Mr. Lokoyome was not able to travel to Sudan then during the December holidays because of the unfavourable political climate back home (Sudan). Sudan, as you may re-call in those years (in the 1970s and 1980s) was a war torn state and travelling was risky and a big problem. Therefore being a colleague at SAUT's School of Journalism and a good friend, I asked him to accompany me to Kenya for his holidays. Mr. Lokoyome was sponsored by the Sudan Council of Churches (SCC). He hailed from Juba in Southern Sudan.

He was a Communications Coordinator at SCC back in Khartoum, Sudan before he came to SAUT. As I was finishing this book for publication I learnt that Mr. Lokoyome was with SCC as Head of Communication.

The Kenyan Security Personnel during their interrogation and torture accused me of working in cohorts with Sudan rebels and that it was on that basis that I sheltered a Mr. Lokoyome in Kenya; an allegation I denied and still deny to-date.

The day (December 15, 1986) when I was picked up by state security agents, I had left Mr. Lokoyome at my residence, Oyugis, for obvious reasons -- to rest as the weekend was hectic after the funds drive, at Kisii Hotel Ltd.

While at my house at Oyugis, I asked the house help to serve the three security agents with some drinks – one of them had remained in the vehicle but was called into the house for a drink. I remember Mr. Araka, a police constable who was the driver, was served with a Sprite soda, while others were served with beers (Pilsner).

The other two police officers drank two beers each. During this time I went about giving some instructions to my wife in our bedroom. At the same time I had an opportunity to change the clothes – I put on a Kaunda Suit (see photograph taken at the Nairobi Law Courts on January 29, 1987, after sentence and conviction below).

Once supper was ready, my wife asked me to join the visitors for supper. At this stage, I was arranging my belongings like clothing, books etc. as any other person preparing to go on safari, and instructed my wife to bring them to Nairobi, which was never to be.

"Where are you going my dear?" My wife asked me. I told her that I was headed for Nairobi. *"Why? You only came back from college through Nairobi last week."* She persisted.

At this point, I decided to explain to my wife the predicament I was in. I at this stage went with her to our sitting room and introduced her to my visitors (read: police officers) with some arrogance and naughtiness in the presence of my Sudanese friend.

I simply told my wife and Mr. Lokoyome that I was asked by this man – in reference to Inspector Kigen, that a Mr. Gerald Ndungu wanted to talk to me in regard to the Saturday December 13, 1986 function at Kisii Hotel.

"Upon arrival at Ndungu's office, he made two or so telephone calls and informed me that I was then under arrest and I was to be taken to Nairobi that same night or the following day, a fact, he said, was to be determined by the Nairobi Office."

My wife immediately asked me, *"What is next?"* I told her that I was to go back to Kisii Police Station with these people (referring to Insp. Kigen and the other two police constables).

Achira and Kamangara at Nairobi Law Courts after their
conviction and sentence on January 29, 1987.

I told my wife and Mr. Lokoyome that Kisii Police Station was where officers, allegedly from Nairobi, who apparently (according to Supt. Ndungu) were to pick me up and take me to Nairobi, where I allegedly committed the offence. At some point, in my house, my wife and Mr. Lokoyome were very uneasy and suspicious and posed a number of questions. *"Why have you been arrested?"* (Mr. Lokoyome would put the questions in English, while my wife in our mother tongue – Ekegusii). *"Do you suspect anything bad or wrong somewhere?"* All my replies to questions raised by my wife and my student colleague attracted the answer *"No."*

My Sudanese friend, at this point was drinking tea, while the police officers were having the drink that had been offered to them. My wife was now nervous and shaky although she wore a strong face and proceeded to serve us with supper which I never ate. My Sudanese friend marvelled at me, for two or so minutes and simply posed one question. *"Jimmy what is it that you suspect that has led to your arrest?"* For the Sudanese, being arrested was not a strange incidence for it was common back home at Khartoum or Juba.

But all the same he appeared worried as I told him; *"My friend Angelo, I am not certain as to why the Kenyan Intelligence have been on me, you see arrests have been common in Kenya in the recent past but I cannot relate or make any connection to those past arrests with my arrest today. Let's not speculate until we get to know the truth as I get to Nairobi tonight or tomorrow."*

All said and done, this time my wife was standing near the door to our bedroom gaping at me and asked one more question in the mother tongue. *"What do you really mean that you don't know?"* She unbelievably shook her head as my little son Douglas emerged from the bedroom; awaken by the talk. Running to me with a wide smile, not knowing that I was under arrest and that he (Douglas) was not going to see me until after two years – when he was three years.

At this point Inspector Kigen signalled to me and asked me that we should go back to Kisii as per the instructions of Supt. Ndungu. Insp. Kigen said that it was getting past time that we were told to be back by mzee (reference to Supt. Ndungu) by 9:00 p.m. It was then approaching 8:45 p.m.

I asked Insp. Kigen to give me some minutes before we would leave for Kisii town. At this point I felt I should leave some money behind with my wife. Indeed the thinking – that I leave some money behind for my wife -- later on worked to be a blessing in disguise as the same money really assisted her to travel to Nairobi to search for me.

For my family, the December 25, 1986 Christmas was not anything good for them to celebrate, for they were not certain where I was. In the house at Oyugis, I took my National Bank of Kenya, Kisii Branch cheque book and wrote two leaves each of Kenya Shillings Two Thousand (2,000.00) for different dates of December 1986 thus, 17th December and 22nd December. I issued the two cheques in favour of my wife and told her to cash the cheques as per the dates or after and that the cash may be of assistance to her in case anything turned to be bad in regard to my arrest.

I was driven to Nairobi on December 17, 1986 in the early hours of the morning. I spent two days (15th and 16th of December) at Kisii Police Station with the Special Branch police offices.

Contrary to Supt. Ndungu's claims that I was to be 'collected' by some officers from Nairobi, he had to escort me with some other plain-clothes police officers to Nairobi. It was a contingent of six police officers in two unmarked police cars. We left Kisii Police Station at 7:10 a.m. for Nairobi. There was a brief stop over at Naivasha for a meal, which I never appreciated, although I took a soda.

CHAPTER TWO

Kisii, Kileleshwa Police Stations

It is 10:35 p.m. when we have arrived at Kisii Police Station from Oyugis Town. Inspector Kigen, who was in-charge during the arrest, handed me over to the police officers who were on duty at Kisii Police Station.

Inspector Kigen instructed the duty officer to take care of me at the station's booking office. I was to wait for the officers who were to come from Nairobi for me that night (December 15, 1986) or the following morning.

"Do not lock him in the cells. Mr. Achira is no 'ordinary Kenyan citizen', just stay with him at the Booking Office as he is waiting for the 'collection' by the officers from Nairobi." Inspector Kigen told the duty officer then.

At Kisii Police Station I knew two of the three police officers who were on duty and I had a brief chat, of course, centered on what had gone wrong that I had to be booked at the station by the Special Branch police.

I had no answer for the question, since I knew nothing. We stayed until about 10:45 p.m. when three friends of mine came to see me at the station, basically to find out what exactly had transpired between Capital Hotel and the Police Station.

The three were Messrs Nyakwara, Omenge and Baraza, whom I was with at the Capital Hotel when Insp. Kigen and his team of plain-clothes police officers came for me as I enjoyed my 'kanywaji' – (small Export Tusker). The three were allowed to talk to me. After chatting, I asked them to bring me some food and they brought chips and roast chicken. My friends left at 11:00 p.m. and came back the following day – December 16, 1986. As in the previous evening, we went through events of the week and explored issues; we got no answer as to why I was picked up by the Special Branch Police and not regular police if not Criminal Investigations Department (CID).

At one point we started to think and suspected that maybe my arrest would be part of the 'crackdown' of the so-called 'political dissidents' though I would not imagine myself one of those who would belong to the alleged group of 'political dissidents'.

However, due to my stand in terms of public issues in regard to politics, I started to be suspicious. All my articles were as controversial as issues of the day in terms of both Gusii and national politics.

All the same I would not imagine myself as one of those who would belong to that group; but due to my controversial articles, news stories, feature articles and commentaries in the *Daily Nation* and *Sunday Nation*, I was left with an option of being suspicious.

While at Kisii Police Station, I sent out an SOS (Save our Souls). I sent word to my lawyer friends in Kisii Town – among them Abuki Omwamba and Reuben Masese of Abuki Omwamba and Advocates and Masese and Co. Advocates respectively.

The message first reached, Mr. Masese. Lawyer Masese, was at the Kisii Police Station at 8:15 a.m., the following day, December 16, 1986. At the police station – just at the back of the station (behind the booking office) lawyer Masese had to assist me in exploring all possibilities – possible options as to why the plain-clothes police had been involved in my arrest.

It took us (lawyer Masese and I) close to one hour, but we never arrived at any definite conclusion as to why I had been picked up by Special Branch police and not any other unit of the police force like CID or regular police. In the end, we were left with no option but to suspect a political hand in play over my arrest.

At the end of my sharing with lawyer Masese we agreed that he would get in touch with my brother – the lawyer, who was then practicing at Eldoret with P.N. Anassi and Co. Advocates. My brother, David Nyakang'o Onyancha was a year-mate and a college-mate (University of Nairobi) of Lawyer Masese. Reason for getting in touch with him, according to Lawyer Masese was to brainstorm and explore various possibilities in regard to my arrest. And in the event of either being taken to court they (Lawyer Masese and my brother, Lawyer Onyancha) would offer legal services.

I also asked lawyer Masese to follow me to Nairobi and find out what would happen to me. After lawyer Masese had left the police station, my wife arrived in the company of some of her friends and brought me breakfast.

My wife was in the company of my little son – Douglas, my maternal cousin Charles Ogechi Migosi and her cousin Annah Aminga.

The police officer on duty allowed my wife to serve me with breakfast. Some friends from the Media fraternity and the Kisii District Information Office also paid me a visit at the police station, with hopes that nothing bad had happened to me.

My wife, relatives and friends were allowed to chat with me. All they did was to wish me well and hoped for good ending and prayed for good tidings ahead of me as I was headed, or destined for Nairobi. The exact destination in Nairobi was not disclosed to me or my relatives. My wife had this to tell me as she bid me goodbye at the police station. *"My beloved husband be brave, have courage, pray hard and bear with the situation and God will see you through the temptations."*

She added; *"As you pray for the best outcome we shall also pray for you, brave the situation and look forward that all will turn out to be well and hope to see you in the same state you have left us."*

Actually, I never saw my wife until January 29, 1987 at the Nairobi Law Courts at about 6:46 p.m. That was exactly 43 days after I left Kisii Police Station on December 17, 1986 for Nairobi in the KWE 547 Land Rover alongside a contingent of six police offices in another unmarked police car.

It was now about 9:45 a.m., as my wife, my cousin Charles Ogechi Migosi and my son Douglas left the Kisii Police Station Booking Office, while other friends had left about ten minutes early. As my wife left, I told her to check on me the following day – December 17, 1986. I imagined that she may find me already having been taken to Nairobi. *"If you find me not present, please get in touch with my brother – Nicholas at Central Bank of Kenya, Nairobi -- to be on the lookout for me in Nairobi,"* I told her.

I also asked my wife to ensure that she followed me to Nairobi and somehow bring with her some clothes for me to change. It was Tuesday December 16, 1986 at Kisii Police Station and I was still waiting to be 'collected' by Nairobi Police, according to Supt. Ndungu.

At about mid-day my eldest sister (read: the oldest of all my sisters and my second follower), Martha Kwamboka Onkoba, rang from her house at Nyangena, Kisii Town – about six kilometers from Kisii Police Station. Since most of the police officers knew me, they had to respond and call me from the cell to talk to my sister.

Earlier, I had overheard Supt. Ndungu give firm instructions to the OCS (Officer Commanding Police Station) that I was not supposed to talk to anybody nor was I to be seen by anybody. True to Supt. Ndungu's instructions, it turned out at about mid-day on Tuesday December 16, 1986, that Supt. Ndungu had instructions from Nairobi not to allow me talk to anybody or to be seen by anybody and that I should be locked in the police cell and wait to be 'collected' by some officers from Nairobi.

Indeed, I was locked up in a police cell alone until the following day when I was escorted to Nairobi by Supt. Ndungu alongside a contingent of six armed plain-clothes police officers. A junior police officer who knew me and was friendly, informed me that there had been firm instructions issued to the OCS by the District Special Branch Officer (DSBO), Supt. Ndungu that I should not be seen or talk to anybody. At the same time, I was to be locked in the cells without failure waiting to be 'collected'.

When I talked to my sister for about five minutes, I told her to inform the other family members that I knew nothing and did not suspect anything in regard to my arrest. It was eight days to Christmas – December 17, 1986, at about 6:25 a.m. I was asked by a police officer who was on duty to come out of my cell at Kisii Police Station. The police officer, who was on duty asked. *"Who is it that is supposed to be taken to Nairobi this morning?"* I suspected it was me, but I did not respond. I deliberately decided to keep silent. After a short while – about three minutes or so, I overheard the voice of the District Special Branch Officer, Supt. Ndungu at the police station's booking office tell the officer on duty that the person's name is Jimmy Achira – the *Nation* journalist.

The officer on duty shouted towards my cell and asked, '*Ni nani Achira hapa ndani?*' (A reference to mean *"who is Achira in this cell?"*) I responded and was ordered to come out of the cell to the booking office. At the booking office I was ordered by the duty officer to put on my personal effects that had earlier been confiscated from me; my shoes, belt, Seiko wrist watch, wallet together with other personal effects were handed back to me. While all this was being done to me, Supt. Ndungu was waiting outside the police station together with his officers and other unmarked police vehicles with six plain-clothes police officers, apparently in readiness to escort me to Nairobi.

When my entire personal effects had been handed over to me, Supt. Ndungu came to the booking office and informed me that we were destined for Nairobi. *"Mr. Achira, the officers who were to come for you are not coming. I have now been asked to take you to Nairobi,"* Supt. Ndungu politely informed me.

He further asked me, *"Do you have anything to do in Kisii before we start our journey to Nairobi?"* I responded, *"Yes. I would like to see my lawyer and talk to him."*

"Who is the lawyer and where?" Supt. Ndungu asked. I told him that it was at Birongo, next to the main road and the lawyer was Mr. Reuben Masese. On the way to Nairobi, Birongo is on the Kisii – Keroka Highway about 18 kilometers from Kisii Town.

Supt. Ndungu allowed me together with his officers to stop at Lawyer Masese's residence, just about 50 meters from Birongo Market. He (Supt. Ndungu) waited in the vehicle (KWE 547 Land Rover) as two officers accompanied me to Lawyer Masese's residence. They (officers) waited outside as I talked to Lawyer Masese – it took me about 15 minutes. I consulted with him on the way forward in regard to my fate. Lawyer Masese's residence, was under plain-clothes police surveillance for about 15 minutes, as people were streaming out of their residences to the main road to travel either to Kisii Town or Keroka Township; wondering what was happening as there were unmarked police vehicles parked outside the lawyer's residence and the entrance (pathway) leading to his house.

At lawyer Masese's residence next to the upper Birongo Market, we found him preparing to take his breakfast and leave for Kisii Town – his law firm offices were that time located at Golf House, Kisii Town. In the house was his wife, who was then a high school teacher at Kisii High School, Kisii District.

Mrs. Masese served us (Police Constable Araka and I) with tea as Ndungu and other officers waited in their vehicles outside the residence. I was somewhat nervous and worried about what was my next fate. I could not finish the cup of tea and the few slices of bread given to me by Mrs. Masese

After consultations, we resolved that he [lawyer Masese] teams up with my brother – David Onyancha, so that they travel to Nairobi to raise the matter with AG, if it took the arresting officers long to produce me in a Court of Law.

December 15 and 16, 1986

For the two days – December 15 and 16 1986, I was at Kisii Police Station -- the experience I had there was unforgettable. It was a short period but horrifying. Several questions were being directed at me by either the police officers on duty or the inmates.

Some obvious questions included: *"Why were you arrested? Who arrested you? Did you steal? Did you rape? Where do you come from? How much money do you have?"*

These kinds of questions among many other questions were posed to me by those in custody waiting to be taken to court. Even the police officers on duty would ask why I had been arrested.

In the police cell there are those suspects who have stayed for three, five, six or so months and seem to be contented with life in general. They are normally very rough and crude in their general conduct. They are not welcoming, unless you concede to whatever questions they ask you.

The questions, some of the police officers and inmates asked me as a journalist reminded me of the style of writing a news story/article.

At the time of my arrest, I had come home for December vacation from college in Tanzania, where I was pursuing my career in Journalism. Therefore the five Ws – (Who, Which, Where, What and When – and the one H which is for How) were still fresh in my mind as a student of journalism.

I at times told the questioners (read: police officers on

duty and inmates) that the questions can be answered if they were asked in an orderly way. This usually generated some small debate and the cells occasionally were like tutorial classes in the journalism course. Even police officers were excited with my lectures on what the five Ws and one H was for. This really assisted me not to be mistreated; instead they (inmates and police officers) demanded to know more about the five Ws and one H.

For the two days I was at Kisii Police Station cells, I had many hours of discussions and at the end most of the silly and stupid questions I was being asked would ordinarily be answered.

At any rate, these silly questions were being asked on the second day – December 1986 in the afternoon and in the night of December 17, 1986.

By the way, for non-journalists, the five Ws and one H are the fundamental basics guiding any budding journalist if he/she has to effectively report an event or incident exhaustively.

This aspect of the five Ws and one H entertained the police officer on duty and suspects on that night of December 16, 1986. They said as I left on the morning of December 17, 1986 – *"We shall really miss you."* Some said *"You should have stayed longer."*

"However, go well and we wish you good" one inmate, who claimed that he had been in remand for six months for stealing a bicycle from his employer said, *"after completion of my case I would want to pursue Journalism as a career."* He was a Form IV school leaver with C- (minus), he claimed.

It was no good as we arrived in Nairobi on December 17, 1986 in the afternoon. We arrived in Nairobi at Nyayo House on the 24th floor if not 25th floor at about 2:25 p.m. I was not sure if it was the 24th or 25th floor, but all the same it was the top most of the towering Nyayo House.

Breakfast in Police Cell

It was 6:00 a.m. in the morning of December 16, 1986 at Kisii Police Station cells. One young man (a suspect), had been allowed into the police cell with a wrist watch that helped me to know what time it was.

It is normally a routine if not a norm that about that time (6:00 a.m.) suspects or inmates in police custody/cells are treated to 'breakfast', which in fact I did not take as much as it was served to me. The inmates were scrambling for the 'breakfast'.

Two of the inmates, who appeared to be very friendly from the time I was locked in the cell, were the beneficiaries of my uneaten breakfast. To date, I remember their names – Jared Osoro from Magena in Gucha and John Okello from Rongo, in Migori District. Osoro told me that he was in custody for theft while Okello was suspected of rape.

That morning of December 16, 1986, my wife brought me breakfast which I was allowed to take by police officers on duty within the booking office. In fact that was the last breakfast I took as a free (citizen) for the folowing two years. The next breakfast I took as a free citizen was at Sakagwa Hotel in Kisii Town in the morning of May 29, 1988. I was released from Kamiti Maximum Security Prison on May 28, 1988 at about 11:25 a.m. through Kisumu's main prison, Kodiaga. By the time I was in Kisumu Town, the clock tower next to Cooperative Bank of Kenya, Kisumu Branch, was reading 12:30 p.m., on May 28, 1988.

Breakfast at the Kisii police cells then was brought in a big plastic bucket and served in plastic mugs which were brought together in a container which appeared like a drum that had been cut half-way.

A middle-built, tall, black man emerged from the cells steel door. As he opened the door aggressively with the help of a duty officer, he was received with shouts from the inmates/suspects. Some of the shouts went like, *"I want to go for a short call."* Others shouting, *"Why do you lock us in throughout the night,"* others begged for drinking water as others shouted in their mother tongues – Ekegusii, Kikuria, Dholuo, Kikuyu and even Kimaasi.

The middle aged man, of course had no time to listen to such shouts or requests, but to concentrate on his duty of serving 'breakfast' – tea and dishing out pieces of loaves.

I was in fact served with a mug of tea and a big slice of a loaf. It was difficult for me to hold the mug, leave alone its smell and in less than a minute there were those who were ready to 'help' me hold it. In fact, I surrendered my 'breakfast' to Osoro and Okello, as mentioned above. The two beneficiaries of my 'breakfast' did appreciate and wished I continued being with them in the cells. They did not take my breakfast alone, but shared with some of their colleagues. When I was leaving in the morning of December 17, 1986, they wished me a safe journey to Nairobi.

It was now 8:15 a.m. on December 16, 1986 and I was still at Kisii Police Station cells. The duty officer, who was to go off-duty at that time, was to check and ensure that he had officially handed over the suspects/inmates to the in-coming duty officer. Confirming the handing over includes physical counting of all the suspects. This is also counter-checked and confirmed by calling out the names of the suspects as recorded in the booking register – Occurrence Book (OB).

Upon calling the names of a suspect, the suspect had to be physically seen and heard responding to his/her name(s) by saying – 'afande'. The essence of calling names and physical counting is to ensure that those who had been booked in the previous day were all present.

Interestingly, I was an exception, for my names were not called. This 'spoilt' the 'hesabu' (mathematics). The duty officer told the incoming duty officer that they had instructions not to enter my names in the Occurrence Book (OB). The officer responded. *"That is unprocedural, for anybody who has been locked in a police cell his/her names must be entered in the OB." "Why is he (read: Achira) an exception?"*

All the same, the incoming officer told me that whenever my names are called I must respond to by saying 'afande'. That morning of December 16, 1986, was the beginning of a norm that was to be part and parcel of me for about two years – by responding to any call directed at me as 'afande'.

I surely found it difficult for the two days I was at Kisii Police Station (December 15 and 16, 1986). Equally, while at Kileleshwa police cells, it was not easy to quickly respond by shouting 'afande'. But I found out the longer one continued staying in the cells, the more he got accustomed to the norms going on in those cells.

While at Kisii and Kileleshwa, if I responded *"yes sir"*, I found the duty officers equally appreciated the response but cautioned me against that saying while in police cell/custody the best response to an officer once your name (referring to me) is called you respond by shouting 'afande'. Once a suspect responds by saying 'afande' they felt (in my view) honoured and indeed they were from that moment friendly. But I came to realize that it is the junior police officers who would prefer for the suspect to respond by saying 'afande'.

I had never really been to a police cell before, except in about three instances while going about my normal duties as a journalist. Sometime, shortly after the attempted overthrow of the Moi/KANU government in August 1, 1982, I was picked up in connection with a news story, I had written and questioned for over six hours. This time I was never locked in the cells, although I spent the hours in the CID offices being interrogated by one Inspector William Oluoch, who was then No.2 in command at the Kisii's CID Offices.

Another time was in Nairobi when I was picked up and booked at Kamukunji Police Station for an overnight stay. But I was released the following day when the duty officer found that I was a journalist with the *Standard* newspapers. The basis of my release was that I was on a news 'night search'.

My response while at Kisii Police cell once my names were called was either 'Yes sir', or 'Present sir'. This appeared to be surprising or unusual for the inmates. Also this was compounded by the fact that I was freely talking to some of the police officers and many people, relatives, friends and colleagues in the media visited me especially in the morning and the first quarter of the morning of December 16, 1986.

At Kisii Police Station, I knew most of the officers by virtue of my public office (journalism). I was at Kisii Police Station cells for about 36 hours. I was booked there at 7:15 p.m. on December 16, 1986, and checked out at 6:35 a.m. on December 17, 1986.

It was at 9:25 a.m., December 16, 1986; I was called from the cell by a duty officer. This time, I was bare-footed. I had no jacket and my hair was uncombed, looking rough, my face was not washed. I really looked a suspect and inmate. But still I tried to be in a relaxed mood and confident as I emerged from the cell, though I was yet to know my fate.

At the Police Station's counter was my wife cradling our son Douglas, my cousin Charles Migosi and dozens of friends. It was unbelievable to many of my relatives and friends, who had been with me that weekend – December 13, 1986 at my high profile function at Kisii Hotel Ltd of raising funds for me to enable me continue with my studies in Tanzania. Some we had not met for a while as I had been a way in Tanzania for my studies and I had come home hardly two weeks before my arrest.

At this point, as I talked to my wife and friends, lawyer Reuben Masese of Masese and Co. Advocates arrived at the station, apparently in response to my appeal through my friends – Messrs Omenge, Nyakwara and Baraza.

It was prudent that I talk to my lawyer. Therefore, I asked my wife and my cousin Charles alongside my other relatives and friends to brave the situation and say prayers for me. They left as I entered into deep sharing with lawyer Masese.

The outcome of my being taken to Nairobi was no good as I ended up at Nyayo House torture chambers through Kileleshwa Police Station, although in the afternoon of December 17, 1986, I was taken to either the 24th or 25th floor of Nyayo House, where Supt. Ndungu was sternly reprimanded for having taken me straight there; instead he should have booked me at any of the Nairobi Area Police Stations until he would receive further instructions. All said and done the outcome was that I was not heard from or seen until January 29, 1987 at about 6:45 p.m. at the Nairobi Law Courts.

This is when I was presented over to the then Chief Magistrate H.H. Buch who with the back-up of one Bernard Chunga handed me over to Kamiti Maximum Security Prison, after jokingly 'convicting and sentencing' me to two years (see *Daily Nation* of January 30, 1987)

At Kisii Police Station on the morning of December 16, 1986, I had the following message for my wife; *"Be strong, courageous confident and never be overtaken by emotions; some patience is great and always remember me in your daily prayers. Also tell the other family members that God has his plans for his creatures"*

At this point, my wife was pensive and looked worried and posed one very cardinal question to me. *"Do you really know why you were arrested?"* I replied; *"I am not anywhere nearer to knowing as to why I am here at Kisii Police Station."* I had five or so minutes of intimate talk or sharing with my beloved son Douglas who was only gaping at me innocently, not knowing that we were going to miss one another for two years.

As I said bye to my wife and my other relatives; I imagined what little Douglas was wondering I was doing there. He could not have understood that I was under arrest. Douglas was then one year and six months old. He was born on June 30, 1985. Wycliffe was not with us for he had joined the grandparents at the rural home for December, 1986 holiday. He was seven years old and in Standard III at Kisii Primary School.

CHAPTER THREE

A Day I Marked in My Life

The day was the 15th day of December, 1986. I got to Kisii Town a few minutes to mid-day and went about my personal and private programmes and activities until about 4:00 p.m., when I decided to have my 'Kanywaji' at what used (then) to be my popular joint – Capital Hotel, right in the heart of Kisii Town. In fact, I arrived in Kisii Town from Oyugis Town (Rachuonyo District), among my activities of the day was to be at Kisii Hotel to facilitate the banking of the money that had been raised by friends and relatives towards my studies that weekend on December 13, 1986 at that same Hotel. But, only to learn that Mzee John Oigara, the proprietor of Kisii Hotel Ltd was to be available in the course of the afternoon. I had kept the cash in the hotel's safe, and the only person who had access to the safe key was the proprietor – Mzee Oigara.

While at Capital Hotel (pub) at about 5:00 p.m., a friend casually whispered to me that some five gentlemen (apparently) policemen from the then dreaded Special Branch Unit were hovering around and about the pub – in the corridors and within the pub. The friend did not stop there; he told me that he overheard them ask a barman – a Mr. Onyango, if I had been seen around. Apparently, when they came I had gone out shortly. But when I came back straight to the counter of the pub, I saw two of them along the corridors leading to the toilets. They greeted me casually as they went away. My thinking, later on, was that they went to report to their boss that I had been seen. After an hour, Insp. Kigen came with his team of five plain-clothes police officers.

When a friend of mine whispered to me that the police were in the pub some time and inquired about my presence, I did not take it seriously. Although right in my heart I got slightly frightened, I did not want to appear scared or frightened.

Why to some extent I got scared deep inside my heart is because that year (1986) and the previous two years (1984 and 1985) the then notorious and dreaded Special Branch Police Unit had been arresting people and torturing suspects of dissenting views forcing them to admit that they belonged to clandestine organizations such as Mwakenya, December Twelve Movement, and Pambana just to list a few.

Just to cut the long story short at this juncture, I will take you to the theatrics and drama at the 24th floor of the then Nyayo House and infamous underground torture cells. The theatrics and drama started on December 18, 1986.

At Nyayo House then the 25th floor, one Gerald Ndungu, who was then the in-charge of the larger Kisii District, holding the portfolio of District Special Branch Officer (DSBO) in the company of one Araka (his official driver) handed me over to the notorious Leonard Wachira, who had been in charge of the arrest of virtually every suspect in connection with the then dreaded Mwakenya and other allegedly related clandestine organizations or movements.

The notorious Wachira at the time of compiling this book (1997-1999), was working at one of the Kenyan Embassies (mission in an African country, while the other notorious colleague of Wachira one Machini had passed on -- may God rest his soul in peace).

At the time of my 'arrest' the late Machini and Wachira worked for the defunct Special Branch police. At the 25th floor of Nyayo House, the Special Branch police boss incharge of Kisii District, who had executed my arrest, was reprimanded over the manner he 'delivered' me to the office.

The straight question from one man, I came to know as Wachira was: *"Why did you have to bring Mr. Achira directly here? You should have booked him at any of the Nairobi Area*

Police stations; and informed us accordingly." Supt. Ndungu, in his rejoinder, pleaded for forgiveness. Immediately, Supt. Ndungu was asked to leave, while Supt. Wachira called me to a small office and informed me that I was to accompany some officers to some place.

As he finished talking some two officers emerged from a room next to where I was seated and asked me to accompany them. As I and the two officers walked along the corridors of 25th floor, two others emerged and accompanied us. We went down the building using a private lift. At this point the officers were four in number.

Where they were taking me, I did not know until we got down and got out of the lift and proceeded to a car park behind Nyayo House Building.

Obviously from their behaviour, since I was used to the Special Branch police officers and their cars, I had no doubt, they were Special Branch. At the car park, one of them told me to enter into a saloon car (Audi, grey) in the back seat. At the back seat I was immediately sandwiched in between two young men, obviously between the ages of 30 and 35 years. In front, of course, were the driver and another officer.

The one in front ordered the driver that we were going to Kileleshwa Police Station. *"This is a criminal and you should not stop anywhere. He needs to be booked at Kileleshwa Police Station cells."* One of them with me at the back seat commented *"Mr. Achira, don't get scared of those statements, you are only going to assist in some matters that we believe their origin is Kisii and that is the only reason why you were brought here."*

In fact, the next destination from the parking bay of Nyayo House was Kileleshwa Police Station and I was booked in the cell. I never saw Supt. Ndungu and PC Araka, although as I was being driven out of Nyayo House parking bay, I saw Supt. Ndungu also being driven out of the same parking yard in his official vehicle – KWE 547, Land Rover long chassis.

The next time, I came to see Supt. Ndungu was when I was working with the Catholic Diocese of Kisii as its Diocesan Communications Coordinator. This time, Supt. Ndungu, I was informed, was stationed at Marsabit still with the Special Branch police.

When I met Supt. Ndungu, it was next to General Post Office, Nairobi. He was with two people and he appeared to be waiting to bode a matatu or a bus headed towards Capital Hill (Community). In fact, I faced him and said *"hello."* He gave the impression of one who was not sure, who was greeting him. I reminded him of my names and his response was, *"Mr. Achira, where are you these days?"*

I gave him a crooked smile and replied, *"You know where you took me to on December 17, 1986. I am back and I am available. Mr. Achira, please forget the past, for you knew what was happening."* I never followed up the statement but proceeded towards Nyayo House, where I was following the renewal of passports of some Catholic priests from Kisii Diocese, who were due to travel at the end of the year for further studies in Rome. I had been sent by the then Bishop of the Catholic Diocese of Kisii, the late Rt. Rev. Bishop Tiberious Charles Mugendi in June 1991.

Back to Kileleshwa Police Station booking office, two of the young policemen who accompanied me from Nyayo House told the duty officer that they were to come for me later on.

The officer on duty instantly raised a complaint. *"You people you have made it a habit that you bring 'suspect(s)' here and you don't follow the laid down procedures. You always want us to book your suspects. What are they suspected of, theft or what?"* The duty officer questioned.

At Kileleshwa Police Station Booking Office, there was some five minutes exchange between the two officers who had taken me there and a duty officer. But, a senior police officer came out of a nearby office and intervened. Apparently, from the ranking, he was a Chief Inspector of Police, and most likely was the Officer Commanding Police Station (OCS). He said *"Put him (referring to me) in the cells and you shall resolve that later."* I was bundled into the cell and in the cell I was alone and as nothing was visible I had to sit on the floor; for I was exhausted after the long journey from Kisii to Nairobi.

It was 3:00 p.m. at Kileleshwa Police Station, Nairobi on December 17, 1986. I was alone in one of the cells. Nobody talked to me until about 7:00 p.m. when a senior police officer – rank of a Chief Inspector, came to my cell. He opened from outside as usual.

He asked me, *"Are you Mr. Achira?"* I replied by saying, *"Yes sir."*

"What are your other names?" I told the officer that my other names were Omwega Achira. *"You are sometimes known as Jimmy Achira?"* I replied, *"Yes."*

The officer asked further, *"Where do you come from?"*

I told him that I came from Nyamira in Kisii District. He asked me what I did for a living.

I told him that I was a student of Journalism, training in Tanzania, but I was (currently) on December holiday. He loudly wondered why I was arrested; and said *"Let's hope that you have not committed any serious crime that warranted the police to bring you all the way from Kisii to Nairobi."*

Then he asked if I had eaten. I told him I hadn't. He assured me that in a short while I was going to be served with a meal. And indeed, he asked the duty officer to ensure that I was served with a meal. In fact, in less than 20 minutes, I was brought ugali and sukuma wiki mixed with some pieces of meat. I was hungry and I had no option but to eat.

Shortly after the 7:00 p.m. news bulletin, one very fat,

bulky, tall black man opened the door leading to my cell. He was in plain clothes and called my names – *"Jimmy Achira, are you there?"* I responded by saying, *"Yes sir, I am in."*

"Come out, we have come for you as you were told." He was right on the door steps of my cell. The accent was of a Kisii -- semi illiterate from his spoken English. I came to know later that he was a driver, attached to Nyayo House Special Squad of Special Branch police team that was designated to arrest suspects of alleged clandestine movements or organizations.

At the booking office of Kileleshwa Police Station, the black, fat, tall driver asked me. *"Are you Jimmy Achira?"* I responded in the affirmative. *"You are the people who want to destroy this good country of ours."* Next to him were three other plain-clothes police officers – who apparently had come to pick me up from Kileleshwa Police Station. Eventually the final destination was Nyayo House basement/cell, a fact I got know after about two weeks!

"Get into the vehicle." It was unmarked white short-chassis Land Rover. As I entered the front and sat next to the driver, the fat, tall man –- whom I came to establish was my kinsman – a Kisii, used the rear opening of the motor vehicle and asked me to come to the back seat.

At the back of the vehicle he told me to lie down on my back. I asked him why I should do so. He then told me in low tones *"don't fear, I am only under instructions by my seniors."* I instantly developed fear and started shivering. *"You are only going to assist in some investigations and you may be released tomorrow."*

As the tall dark man was instructing me to lie down on my back, two other plain-clothes police officers, apparently Special Branch police, who appeared to be in charge, got closer to the vehicle and ordered the driver to speed up for the journey was a long one. I was blindfolded and instantly ordered to lie on my back and not to raise my head at all.

Although blindfolded, I could tell that the driver was driving in the direction of Westlands. And at one stage I got to know that we were getting through Waiyaki Way in Westlands. After some distance, I remotely saw us enter Kabete Police Station. At Kabete police station parking bay, it was ensured that I was well blindfolded. We were there for about 30 minutes or so. Two other people were brought into the same Land Rover. I am not sure, but I believe they were also suspects and blindfolded.

After, I was joined by two other (suspects). I believe the driving took over 30 minutes, and I realized we were at the Jomo Kenyatta International Airport (JKIA) because I slightly managed to dislodge the blindfold sneakily. While there, I overheard one of the officers give instructions as they walked to the parking bay – "*you will take the longest route to Buru Buru Police Station, where we shall pick up two other criminals.*"

Still totally blindfolded, I overheard one of the officers saying, "*get those two people from Nakuru whom we left here yesterday.*" The officers did not mention the names of the suspects. It was after close to two hours, since we had left JKIA.

After about three and half hour drive from Kileleshwa Police Station through Lavington, Westlands, and Kabete Police Station to the airport and back through Buru Buru Police Station in Eastlands, Nairobi through the city centre, the Land Rover stopped after going through some kind of downhill of an enclosed area. In fact, this was now Nyayo House basement area cells/dungeons).

As the Land Rover stopped with a bang, a steel gate was opened, apparently with a lot of force and locked up again. I knew it was a basement or underground of a building for the Land Rover was being driven slowly and carefully. I was in no doubt that we were in an underground parking. However, I was not able to say where. After a couple of days, I came to know that it was at Nyayo House basement.

At the underground parking, two men led me through a corridor of about 10 to15 feet before a room was opened also with force like the gate where the Land Rover was allowed entry. This was now not the gate, but a door leading to a dry cell in the underground basement of Nyayo House.

I was put in an empty, dark, dry cell with no window; I was unblindfolded and left in the cell. In the cell, there was a mattress. The two people who led me to the cell, one said, *"You sleep there and we shall come for you later."* As I was being led to the room, I heard some rooms being closed within the same area and some rooms being opened.

"When are you coming back for me?" apparently a suspect asked. I came to learn later on that it was the voice of one John Maina Kamangara, late politician-cum-activist. Kamangara later died after a while following his release from Kamiti Maximum Security Prison, Nairobi.

Dark Cell at Nyayo House Basement

In the dark cells at Nyayo House basement, I was extremely exhausted and it was not possible to imagine where I was.

However, after a while I went into deep sleep on the mattress though there was no blanket or bed sheet to cover myself up. I deeply slept until I was woken up to be served with 'breakfast', in the morning of December 18, 1986. I was served with a cup of tea and one big piece of loaf. The gentleman who served me politely said, *"Take that breakfast and wazee watakuja kuongea na wewe baadaye"* ("Take that breakfast and the elders shall soon come to talk to you over some issue.") Apparently in reference to police officers who were charged with interrogating suspects and were located at the 24th and 25th floors of the towering Nyayo House Building. In the morning, two men came and violently knocked on the door of my cell, and asked me to open but it was not possible. The doors, I learnt later, were like the rest in the police station cells thus were opened from outside.

After a while the door was opened from outside. The impression given to me was that the officers did not want me to recognize them. As the door was being opened, one of them told me to face the wall, while one did the job of blindfolding me. Upon blindfolding me, I was led to an office where I was given a chair to sit on while still blindfolded. I realized that I had used a lift and I was in some small office and indeed I had been put in a lift accompanied by an officer while blindfolded.

On arrival at this small office on the 24th floor of Nyayo House, I was unblindfolded. In front of me was a plain-clothes policeman, whom I came to know later as Chief Inspector Peter Karanja. He asked me, *"Mr. Achira, you are here because you were out to cause chaos in this good country. Do you agree?"* I told him, *"Not that I know of what you are talking about."*

At this point, Chief Inspector Karanja told me, "If you don't know, you are going to face wazees who know all about your activities and you shall then tell them." Before, I replied to CIP Karanja's statement, one person emerged from next office and blindfolded me without uttering a word and led me to another room within the same floor of the building.

In this room I was unblindfolded and the room looked like conference hall or a big board room with four long tables and chairs. Seated was a dozen plus well fed and tough-looking middle-aged men. Coming out conspicuously tall, fat, and with a small head and pitch black was James Opiyo, as I came to know him later.

The famous, or infamous, James Opiyo, depending who you are, apparently was the Chief Interrogator. He looked at me right on my face and shouted at me *"Welcome Mr. Achira, the Chief Public Relations Officer of Mwakenya. Mr. Achira, do you know why you are here today? And are you aware why you were arrested in Kisii and brought here? We want you to be honest and sincere by answering the*

41

following questions. If you correctly and rightly answer the questions to the satisfaction of these officers, we shall have no objection but to release you for you know well that you must go back to college in Tanzania for your studies." He (read: Opiyo) further went on to apologize that his officer both in Kisii and Nairobi had kept me too long knowing well that I was a student on holiday. He, to some extent condemned them. But all turned out to be their style of doing or conducting their affairs.

At this point in time, I got so frightened and concluded that all was not well and now I had been grouped, or rather classified, in the group of dissidents I had read about in the Press. Being detained or jailed for being members of clandestine organizations such as December Twelve Movement, Pambana and Mwakenya.

However, I comforted myself and faced a dozen plus fat, stout looking men. At this stage some of them were reading newspapers, others busy chatting amongst themselves, while some appeared unconcerned with what Opiyo was asking me. Apparently the questions were precisely five. Following are the five questions:

1. When did you join "Mwakenya?"
2. Who recruited you to the movement?
3. When did you take the "Mwakenya oath?"
4. Who was the administrator of the oath? And who were present at the ceremony?
5. Where did your oathing ceremony take place or where was it conducted?

Immediately, after asking the questions, without waiting for an answer, Opiyo implored me to answer the questions without fear. *"If you answer all the questions, you will only be the state witness against those who recruited you and administered the oath, for they are already in police custody,"* Opiyo told me.

In fact, I did not want to answer the questions. All I told him (Opiyo) was that I knew nothing about Mwakenya, except from the reports I read in the press. *"How is that possible and you are in Tanzania? Are you not the Coordinator and Liaison Officer of Mwakenya in Tanzania?"* Opiyo asked me.

I got startled and surprised at this point in time. At this stage all the men were now gaping at me and two of them shouted at me by saying, *"Be honest and tell us the truth or else you leave this place in a coffin. Do you know how many people have died here and nothing is done or has been done to us? We are the state and the legal government you have been planning through Mwakenya to overthrow,"* one officer shouted at me, holding a pistol on his left hand and pointing at me right in my face.

Once more, I sternly looked into Opiyo's face and told him; *"I don't know anything about what you are asking in regard to Mwakenya."*

"We have tangible evidence of your (referring to me) activities, programmes and involvement in Mwakenya, and how you went to Tanzania. Your activities in Tanzania in regard to Mwakenya are well known to us; you know we are the government agents. Tell us the truth and the truth shall set you free."

I, at this point in time, had the courage and said; *"Wazee all the questions you have asked me, I am sorry to tell you that I know nothing about Mwakenya, apart from what I have read in the Press and what I have heard from the electronic media."*

"What is it that you refer to as electronic media?" One interrogator asked.

"I mean radio and TV."

The seemingly annoyed Opiyo barked at me. *"I do not want to hear anything from you. You are as defiant as your fellow colleagues. Just remove all your clothes."* I hesitated and all I got were very sharp blows and kicks from one of the 'wazees' who shouted at me *"We are not here to waste our time! Do as you have been ordered to do, remove all your clothes!"*

As I removed my clothes, one of the wazees remarked with laughter, *"You can see the pants he is putting on. They are those of Mwakenya members, which they normally wear when they prepare to administer the oath."* They (officers) laughed almost in a chorus, an acknowledgement to their colleague's remarks.

As they laughed, I stood stark naked in front of a dozen plus men, one of them apparently a Kisii (my tribesman) who was well-known to me and we would meet (in the past and before my arrest) in social places in Nairobi and Kisii. He appeared shy and withdrawn in the entire episode. But, at some point during the middle of the interrogation he left the interrogation room. He never showed up until some day when he came to make an inquiry from one of my interrogators – Supt. Francis Ndirangu, who was then based at Nyahururu, but was in the 'Crack Unit' at Nyayo House headed by Supt. James Opiyo, as I came to know later.

The notorious James Opiyo, after I stripped myself and remained naked, ordered me to touch the ground with my fore-finger and start moving in a circle, while the other tough-looking men were taunting me and making fun of my anatomy.

At the same time the men were beating me with broken pieces of wood bands made out of worn out motor vehicle tyres. After about eight to ten rounds, I just collapsed as a result of the pain and exhaustion. This time around, the policemen in the "interrogating panel" were just laughing at me and alleging that I had 'cuts' on some parts of my body, and this was done when I was taking the Mwakenya oath.

At one stage, I was ordered by Opiyo to do push-ups. I did fewer than eight and collapsed again. Upon collapsing, they (officers) claimed, *"Those are tactics of Mwakenya followers, wake him up."* Waking me up was by being descended upon by blows, kicks and slaps together with broken pieces of wood. I, at this point, despaired and concluded that I was there (at Nyayo House 24th floor) to die and dared the Chief Interrogator by candidly addressing him as I was seated on the floor of the interrogation room. *"Mr. Opiyo, at your age you are more or so the age-mate if not age bracket of my father, who does not know where I am now. I am your son and imagine your son being in the position I am right now. You and your colleagues have decided to torture me for no apparent reason. What you are doing to me is only to serve your personal ego and greed, for you know well that I don't belong nor do I know what Mwakenya is all about."*

"You as a father, you know well you are cheating and you are out to sacrifice me because of my controversial reportage from Kisii as a Nation Correspondent, and probably I have annoyed some people in the system or corridors of power."

"Don't talk to us that way young man" one of the officers shouted at me as I maintained addressing them and indeed they listened to me.

One would see from their body language that they (officers) were moved by my speech.

I continued: *"You well know that I am a self-sponsored student of journalism at Nyegezi Social Training Institute, Mwanza, Tanzania, where I have been the past year studying. You then deliberately cheat the world that I am at Arusha, Tanzania coordinating activities of Mwakenya a claim which is not true and much unfounded. I know nothing about Mwakenya, apart from Press reports about the movement may God guide me if I am saying the truth. Equally, may God bless you if you are saying the truth about me and my (if any) involvement in the movement."* I closed my address (speech) at this point.

At this juncture, I realized that some of the "interrogating officers" in the panel were moved by my testimony, although two of them, immediately after I finished my address, physically pinned me on the floor and whipped me several times accusing me of being arrogant, defiant and disrespectful to the officers.

At this stage as the two officers whipped me, I constantly yelled and shouted: *"God will punish you and your families for being liars and cheats and accusing me unfairly before the eyes of God. I have never been a member of a clandestine organization as alleged by you."*

"Take him back to rest and he may think over the questions I asked him (referring to the five questions posed to me at the start of interrogation) and you shall continue with him later," Opiyo ordered.

At this stage, I was virtually unconscious lying flat and stark naked on the floor. I was terribly exhausted. I could not manage to stand upright. I was in pain over my entire body. Opiyo ordered, saying: *"take him back and do as usual if he is not cooperating."* Some two young men in their thirties emerged from the next room. I was instantly blindfolded and led to a lift then down to the basement dungeon at Nyayo House basement.

Before I was blindfolded and taken back to the dungeons, one officer ordered me to dress up. I dressed up and I was then blinded, and taken away from the interrogation conference room on the 24th floor of the Nyayo House.

At the dungeons, I was ordered to undress and my clothes taken away. After about 20 minutes, I was taken to another cell where I found two men who directed a hose pipe of cold water at me before the cell was flooded with water to the ankle level. The water from the hose pipe was pretty cold and it really assisted to cool down the pains I was inflicted with during the beating at the 24th and 25th floors. I constantly prayed to my God for Opiyo and his team to spare my life and appealed to the Almighty to touch their hearts and ask them to refrain from outright lies and cheating before God's eyes.

Although the hose pipe water helped to ease the pain inflicted on my body I really felt it. A similar process was repeated over and over again for about 20 days. I appeared before the Opiyo panel of three persons – Leonard Wachira, Francis Ndirangu and Peter Karanja; although Mr. Karanja was the person who was to interrogate me up to the end. In fact, he was the one together with Chief Insp. Jacob Katama, who took me to court for conviction and sentence after 45 days at Nyayo House basement dungeons.

In essence, the line of interrogation by the three men, and a Mr. Karanja, was that I should not have been difficult, for that would waste my time. They urged me to make a confession and spare myself the problems at Nyayo House and go back to college in Tanzania. My interrogators would tell me of many who had died in their hands (refer Special Branch and Criminal Investigating police) and nothing was done to them; and they (victims) were just easily forgotten.

All through I insisted that I had nothing to confess. My three interrogators tried one trick on me –- you confess and we take you to court where you shall be released, for you are a student and you were only suspected. They even told me of my brother (Nicholas Abuga Achira) who was then an employee of Central Bank of Kenya (CBK) and my uncle – Hon. David Onyancha, who was then my local MP (West Mugirango) that they have agreed to pay the court fine for me. The court fine my interrogators said was Kshs 4,500.

I suspected all they told me was a trick to have me accept and be taken to court. Fine, my brother and my uncle were then working at CBK and as an MP respectively, but that did not convince me.

Lastly, I was tricked by one officer (interrogator) who said, *"Now that Mr. Achira you have stayed with us over one month we shall only release you through a court of Law by getting non-custodial sentence and at least a manageable court fine of about Kenya shillings 5,000."*

The interrogators asked me to plead guilty for being a member of a clandestine movement. And in fact, a charge was drafted to that effect. I knew it was pure lies and that those were all tricks played to pin me down like all other alleged Mwakenya accomplices or suspects.

At this point in time, in fact, I was convinced beyond a doubt that I was headed for prison/detention. I was clear in my mind and convinced that prison or detention was a better option than being kept indefinitely at Nyayo House torture chambers and dungeons.

The brutal and animalistic torture and treatment by the Opiyo squad was no more my choice. I knew I was headed for Kamiti Maximum Security Prison with no less than five years. I consoled myself and agreed to confess.

When I was taken to court before Chief Magistrate H.H. Buch, I knew I was about to start prison life hence being 'guest of the Government'. I kept my part of the bargain while the police did not. I was sentenced to two years in jail and saw my interrogators and the Chief Prosecutor, Bernard Chunga, laugh so hard, for they had realized their objective. Chunga was later on to become the Chief Justice of Kenya.

In fact, it goes without saying that Chunga was designated then to conduct prosecution on all Mwakenya, Pambana and December Twelve Movement related cases, whereas certain magistrates were specifically detailed to hear the same cases.

Indeed, it was the criteria that the Moi-KANU government applied in rewarding some officers in the judiciary. Those who heard and imprisoned or fined culprits of such cases were promoted. No wonder Chunga ended up being the Government top man in the judiciary. Chunga became Chief Justice, but was 'bundled' out of office by pressure from the public following the departure of Moi-KANU administration after December General Elections of 2002.

He resigned before the National Rainbow Coalition (NARC) administration took action against him.

45 Days of Torture Sessions

The defunct Special Branch police, I recall well, were led by Insp. Kigen, who later became an ACP (Assistant Commissioner of Police), attached to the Rift Valley Province, Deputy Provincial Special Branch Officer, which later on was disbanded and replaced by the NSIS (National Security Intelligence Services).

After over 24 hours in the closed, wet cell with a dim lighting system from one side of the tall wall, I lost track of events. I would not know when it was day or night, the dates, nor was I able to make out the difference between day and night.

I only came to know that it was January 2, 1987 while undergoing interrogation in one of the rooms. My interrogators a Wachira and a Ndirangu had a copy of the *Daily Nation* and I managed to glance at it and saw the dates.

Now, after about two days, I was subjected to serious sessions of stage managed confessions extracted from equally tortured victims, who claimed they knew me and that I had taken an oath with them, and attended meetings with them.

They further claimed that I had been involved in receiving and entertaining Mwakenya agents while in Dar es Salaam, Tanzania and at times in Mwanza and Arusha. The torture sessions and stage managed confession sessions went on until I got used to the interrogators.

Now, it came the fortieth day and I was to be taken to court to be 'formally charged' and be released, but I was reluctant to say if I would enter a plea of guilty. This made my interrogators to delay for another three days.

Again in the morning of the forty-third day, I was asked if I was ready. I told my interrogators that I was ready to enter a "plea of guilty" because they wanted it to be so. They menacingly beat me up and said that it was to my advantage to enter a plea of guilty, for I was to be released and that the only punishment I was to receive was a fine of Kshs 6,000 and be allowed to proceed to Tanzania to complete my journalism course.

It excited me that I would be allowed to travel to Tanzania and continue with my journalism studies.

At the same time, I convinced myself that even if I was not released, but convicted to go to prison, it was a better option than being at Nyayo House Police Station's torture chambers and cells/dungeons.

On the forty-fifth day, I was blindfolded as usual in the morning and bundled into a lift with the assistance of an officer up to 25th floor of Nyayo House.

In this case, I was taken to Opiyo's office and present were my two interrogators – Wachira and Ndirangu. Opiyo lectured me for close to 30 minutes on how my life can be spoilt and that I am a young person with a bright future in school. He even told me that I had a young family that needed me and my parents had invested in me in terms of education and they were waiting for my fruits.

Opiyo, at this point, I would see in between his lecture that he was yet to convince me to plead guilty, for I had stayed with them at Nyayo House longer than they expected.

Opiyo further told me that it would be illegal to release me without going through the court of law. Once I appeared before the court, and that I will be fined and be released immediately, for his officers and he had made those arrangements and that I shall only be fined Kshs 6,000. He told me that the fine shall be paid by the government. He added, *"One of your relatives has been informed and shall be in the court then to receive the Kshs 6,000 from one of my officers."* (Meant to be shortly before the commencement of the court process).

Opiyo, as cunning as he was, he in fact mentioned names of my relatives whom he claimed to have talked to and they were to be in court during my appearance. He at same time listed the names of my relatives in the public service and political circles.

From the look of events and the stage-managed session spearheaded by Opiyo, the head of the dreaded defunct Special Branch police unit, I was given an opportunity to respond. I very well knew that all that Opiyo had told me, although seeming to be convincing, was all lies, but I admitted that I was going to enter plea of guilty; which indeed I did. That was the start of my custodial sentence of 24 months!

At this stage, I was handed over a well-digested and written mitigating statement which underscored the factors that made me to join the clandestine movement-Mwakenya. I went through the statement and as if in approval, I shook my head, and at this point Opiyo appeared to have done his part and told me to accompany my two interrogators to a room on the 25th floor. Opiyo pretentiously appeared apologetic to all that had happened to me during the torture sessions at Nyayo House Chambers and apologized on behalf of his team then wished me a good and safe journey back home (Nyamira) and to St. Augustine University to complete my studies.

In the room, my interrogators were equally apologetic and from their faces one would be convinced that they were sincere to their heart.

I personally was left with no doubt in my mind that all was lies and I was headed for prison or detention. The two interrogators became friendly, saying, *"You abide with what mzee (read: Opiyo) has told you and things shall go on well."* (Read: you shall be freed!).

I knew all these were tactics, tricks and niceties of the dreaded Opiyo team, but I did not want to appear having not taken the message seriously. The following day – a Thursday (January 28, 1987) I believed it was shortly after lunch, I was brought my red short sleeved shirt, grey Kaunda suit, spectacles, shoes, socks, pants, belt and handkerchief.

Early, I had firm instructions to shower and comb my hair. In fact, I was given Vaseline (body oil) for my face and hands. I was told to get ready for the release in the afternoon as per mzee's (Opiyo's) instructions.

Honestly, I convinced myself that all was not going to be well, for I had heard stories of similar incidents, while in custody for the 44 days.

Come afternoon, two men plus one of my interrogators -- Wachira -- came to the cell and made sure that I dressed up well, combed my hair, vaselined (oiled) my face and actually my brown shoes were polished. In fact I had a good lunch compared to the past. The three were looking on and all through they appeared very friendly.

At about 4:45 p.m., I was once more blindfolded and gently pushed into the Land Rover then driven out of the Nyayo House basement. I realized (from the voice) that one of my "colleagues" – was accompanying me in the vehicle.

I later on at the courts got to know it was John Maina Kamangara, a Nakuru politician, who was handed down a jail term of 15 months.

At the Nairobi Law Courts cells, my interrogators, who appeared not to be sure of the results of my appearing in court that afternoon, came to the cell at the court's basement. *"Mr. Achira, you know it is about time for you to appear before the magistrate, we still hope you will abide with what you agreed with mzee."* The term "mzee" here was in reference to Mr. Opiyo.

I smiled and responded that I would abide by what Mr. Opiyo wanted me to do, but I know eventually I am going to prison. No! No! No! Wachira (read: interrogator) appeared very shocked that I may change the plea to not guilty. I responded to him; *"Be assured that I shall plead guilty."* And indeed I did it before the late Chief Magistrate, H.H. Buch. It was about 6:45 p.m. The journey to Kamiti started -- that was the happiness and joy for Opiyo and his team.

Nyayo House Torture Chambers and Aftermath

The account of my arrest and torture may sound to many of you like the hallucinations or product of my fertile imagination, for it is difficult to envision the then Special Branch police using all methods of torture –- physical and psychological -- on a fellow Kenyan just to force a confession.

Those, however, who were caught in the web set up by the police to catch perceived dissidents in the 1980s, will confirm my account as being an accurate and vivid record of events at Nyayo House torture chambers, cells and dungeons.

Just in passing, there are those who experienced it and they are presently in public life, while some are leading quiet and private lives (see the roll of horror of those who went through Nyayo House Police Station torture chambers elsewhere in this book). The list of those who went through the chambers is so long that what is contained in this book is not exhaustive).

The Nyayo House torture chambers routine was being held in solitary confinement, stripped naked and ridiculed, beatings, threats, inducements, starvation, and being hosed with cold water and left in water-logged cells for several hours while naked without food.

The physical and mental effects of all the torture and forced confessions for crimes never committed tend to generate everlasting trauma. For example, there were several charges made against me, some based on laughable evidence, real and imaginary. The charges stretched back to the early eighties (1980s) when I was a very active journalist with the Nation Group of Newspapers.

For instance, it was claimed that some of the stories I wrote about Kenyan leaders were aimed at undermining the legitimately and legally constituted government of Kenya, then led by Moi. It was also claimed that I had been sponsored to go to Tanzania to pursue further studies in journalism so that I would come back and be in charge of the media in Kenya, once the dissidents took over the Moi-led Government.

The allegation was based on the fact that I used to champion and write about the rural people and their problems – poor transport infrastructure, schools with poor facilities, inadequate and dysfunctional health facilities, as well as poor services to farmers.

This made my interrogators to conclude that I had communist views or thinking. In fact, I was only championing the plight of the rural populace and wrote stories which would assist the government to take some action. The stories, to my dismay, were classified as anti-government and against both the regional and national leadership.

The other alleged evidence of my being dissident was the fact that I chose and went for my journalism studies in Tanzania, a country then seen as socialist leaning. While my main sponsors, who were the then Kitutu East MP (now Kitutu Masaba) Hon. Abuya Abuya, and Hon. Mashengu wa Mwachofi (then Wundanyi MP), were perceived as anti-establishment.

In fact, the two former MPs were among the guests of honour during my *harambee,* which was held at Kisii Hotel, to raise funds to enable me pursue my studies in journalism at St. Augustine University of Tanzania (SAUT) School of Journalism.

At the torture chambers there was a police officer who, every morning, would visit the 'dissidents' at their cells and pose one question in Kiswahili. *"Uko na neno unataka kuambia wazee?"* ("Do you have any word/message that you want to tell the interrogators?").

At the Nyayo House torture cells/dungeons, survivors/ victims can well recall the man who came to be known as *"Una maneno ya kuambia wazee?"* He was the man who, every morning, opened the door a jar and uttered the above words. In fact all he meant was; *"Do you have anything to tell the elders,"* in other words, *"Do you have anything to confess to the interrogators."*

If your reply was negative the old man slammed the door shut to return the next morning, or after a while, to ask the same crude question. Occasionally, I personally would respond positively. The next move was to be blindfolded and bundled into the interrogation rooms or chambers on the 25th floor; your interrogators anxiously waiting for some news. If you had no "substantive news", you were beaten and sent back to the cells at the basement.

The standard warning and inducement given by the Nyayo House police team can be summed up like Dr. Wanyiri Kihoro did it in his book, 'Never say die - the chronicle of a political prisoner', it went like:

"You are not cooperating with our investigation...

"You are not telling us what we want to hear.

"You are keeping everything to yourself.

"You don't want to betray your friends. You had better know one thing though, that you must tell us everything about them.

"If you want to get out of here (torture chambers) *soon, we have got your file, which has everything about your activities. Do not wait until we start unearthing those things because if this happens, we will not be in the best of moods afterwards. You must tell us all, everything and then you shall be free."*

Basically, the interrogators wanted to be told what they wanted to hear and not necessarily the truth. They claimed they had evidence against you (suspect) and yet did not prosecute. As for freeing those who told all, there is no evidence.

CHAPTER FOUR

Jail Was a Better Option

On January 29, 1987 at about 7:00 p.m., we arrived at Kamiti Maximum Security Prison, Nairobi under tight security. This point in time, James Opiyo and his "Nyayo House Police Station torture squad" were not there. It was only the prison warders or jailers for that matter.

I was in the company of one Nakuru politician, John Maina Kamangara and a few prison convicts, less than ten.

Politician Kamangara had been convicted and sentenced to 15 months for failing to report that "a secret movement was publishing and printing a seditious publication". For Kamangara it was alleged that he participated in publishing and printing, which took place between January 1985 and December 1986.

He (Kamangara) had failed to report the activities which were within his knowledge. I had also been convicted and sentenced to two years for "being a member of the secret movement between October 1981 and December 15, 1986." On arrival at the main gate, I was not aware of where we were being taken; all I knew was that we were headed for prison after less than minute court trial that started at 6:15 p.m. at Nairobi Law Courts.

At Kamiti the gigantic iron gate was opened and banged shut and the air of confinement hung heavily on the atmosphere (this time we were still in the prison lorry). Here, resignation and despair ruled the air.

At Kamiti Prison's compound (documentation office), the walls, the barbed wire and the iron gates built a house of separate terror; a terror of confinement, hostility from the warders was all over, the faces of the jailers were self-telling that you are an enemy, their prey, a man who was about to overthrow their "beloved government, under the wise leadership and stewardship of His Excellency President Daniel Arap Moi."

Still at the documentation office with the barbers hard on us, shaving us clean, the walls were very high and heavy metal doors separated us (prisoners) from freedom and the rest of the world. The walls had razor wires on top that sealed us (inmates) in.

Behind those walls, wires and doors, there was a yearning to reach out to the world beyond. Pairs of eyes peered out into the light at fellow inmates, yet others stood in solitary poise. You are not free to walk as you please. You are always under guard. Talking as you please and living as you please became a thing of the past. You eat when it is time to eat. You sleep when the bell goes. You wake up when the bell goes and you bathe at the appointed hour -- if you are lucky two times a week, otherwise once.

You cannot decide to walk across to the shop to buy yourself a cigarette as that is prohibited. You cannot telephone a friend or a relative when you have the urge (remember you have no access to such facilities in the first instance). You don't have a phone; you cannot decide. You are not free. You are deprived of all your freedom.

Everything in prison is routine, orderly and well programmed. Rules must be followed. This structured living stretches one's resilience to the limit.

It brings to mind the words of Eldridge Cleaver: *"In prison, those things withheld from and denied to the prisoner become precisely what he wants most of all. But in a place where life stretches long and hard, needing something one cannot get becomes acid poured on an open wound."*

Journalist Mildred Ngesa of *Society* - a pull-out in *Sunday Standard* wrote: "Visits are probably the only thing that keeps a prisoner going. If lucky, once after a long time, a relative or a friend drops by to find out how you are doing. In only 15 minutes of talking to a loved one, even a prisoner on death row can 'live again'". That is the general glimpse of all until you get to know it by yourself. Do you want to know it? Ask to go there. There are many ways on how you can get to prison and you'll get to know all about it.

My Experience at Kamiti and Kodiaga

Kenyan prisons and remand homes are primitive places by all standards. Staying alive, leave alone keeping one's dignity, is in itself a considerable feat - to successfully complete your jail term alive requires strength and courage.

Many do not successfully complete the jail term, some die in the remand, while others die in the prison. It is a horrifying experience to be a guest of the state by either being remanded or sentenced to serve a prison sentence.

Often, one reads in the newspapers that so and so has been remanded for a period of time, awaiting trial or sentencing. Equally, there are or there were times when one read in the local newspapers that politician so-and-so or journalist X was yesterday or over the weekend picked up for questioning or interrogation for that matter. "Efforts to confirm with the police where the culprit was were fruitless."

In all these cases, the culprit or suspect ends up at a police station and is booked at the Occurrence Book (OB) and bundled into the police cell.

Ordinarily, all police cells are primitive, dirty to sleep in or stay. Besides that, one's dignity is lost once you get to a police cell or remand. And for the defunct Special Branch police unit, they are dungeons (many of them in fact are under-ground cells).

In custody, the practice is to be woken up alongside with other remandees at the same police cell and other neighbouring cells. The wake-up call is followed with the order: 'Hesabu'- meaning everyone has to be in place bunched up in lines of four or five, ready to be counted.

It is only after 'hesabu' that a remanded person can hope to be rewarded with a breakfast of either porridge or tea splashed with milk and at times with a slice of a loaf and nothing else. It is important that the counting goes well for if it does not, the process has to be repeated; several times until it is correct.

If it is in prison, it is different from a police cell. All at prison have to be, in most cases, if not all, naked. Believe it or not stark naked! Never mind that these remandees represent all ages –- ranging from 18 years to 70 or 80 years.

There are those who would see nothing odd having remandees or prisoners huddled together, nude. However, in most African cultures, it is unheard of for an elder to be seen naked by his children. For a 50 year old man, this will mean anyone below the age of 30 years.

For those not familiar with prison jargon, a 'tero' is a commando type warder with the ostensible goal or target of eliminating the use of contraband or banned items (referred to as 'marufuku').

Ordinarily; items considered 'marufuku' are to name a few; sugar, cigarettes, bhang, belts, newspapers or newspaper cuttings, writing material, watches, books, magazines and any food from outside - the list is endless. These raids are no doubt well intentioned, although the way they are executed is indefensible.

The irony in these efforts is that the same warders who are employed and deployed to carry out the 'raids' are the ones actively involved in smuggling these banned (marufuku)' items into the prison. In any event, none really believes that there is any genuine attempt to stamp out the smuggling or bringing illegal contraband to prison.

Raids are carried out as a means of extorting money from those in charge of prison blocks, or revenge for those who refuse or neglect to contribute the bribes --'tithes' -- demanded mainly by the ranked warders (read: chief officer 1 and above).

Ordinarily, it is claimed that raids are carried out as a means of raising much needed capital for the Major or Corporal in charge of such raids. While 'teros' are quite a common occurrence, although many long serving remandees commonly referred to as 'trustees' are not frequent as they used to be for the ordinary remandees or prisoners; similar raids can be carried out two or three days in succession.

From what is conducted or carried out in remands and prisons, it would therefore appear that while the rest of the country and the world is moving towards reforms, prison authorities have engaged a reverse gear and are determined in taking inmates back to the old dark ages.

The question, I would ask myself, and which I am sure every remandee or prisoner would cry out for an answer from those in charge of remand prisons, is: Why is it necessary to continue with this dastardly and dehumanizing practice?

A Typical Prison Day Starts At 5:00 AM

A typical prison day starts at around 5:00 a.m. But on weekends and national holidays they begin a little later at 7:00 a.m. The first call one hears is *'Amka', 'Hesabu'*, and *'Watu wakabe mara moja'*, meaning 'Wake up; squat and get ready for counting' (read: physical counting).

Once it is 'wake up' and 'squat' for 'hesabu', no one is allowed to go for a call of nature. You have to line up, inside your prison block, in lines of four or five, squatting with hands behind your heads!

The wake-up call for counting is normally triggered either by sighting of one or two officers carrying clip board(s). At times the prisoners and remandees have to rely on a series of bells rang between 4:45 a.m. and 6:00 a.m. When the third and the last bell goes, you all have to be ready for counting popularly known as 'hesabu'. The hesabu is carried out by two officers of normally the rank of corporal or above. At times of crisis, officers of the ranks of Chief Officer I or II (COI/II), the equivalent of Chief Inspector or

Supt. of Police (for the case of the police force) or above may be involved.

Once the *'hesabu'* is concluded, 'breakfast' is served. Normally it comprises of porridge.

The prisoners or remandees are released by blocks to collect their share or ratio. When all the members of one block have received their ration, they are taken back and locked up again in their prison cell for they may be tempted to go for the second ratio.

There are normally very sad incidents as some prisoners insist on getting double rations. Because of insisting to get it, they normally receive some serious beatings from the warders on duty. But this does not deter some of them from going for the double rations. Such prisoners are ordinarily referred to by warders and fellow prisoners as 'wezi wa uji' or 'ugali' (porridge or ugali thieves).

In many cases, if not all, the ration given out at prison or at remand cell is by all standards grossly inadequate. Almost every day except national or public holidays and weekends, there are prisoners who have made an appeal against sentence and conviction or the remandees whose cases are being heard. Those going to court are assembled at a yard, where they are sorted out for transportation to different courts. And those who are not going to court are locked up.

In most cases, there are three lots/dispatches of prisoners or remandees to Kibera, Makadara courts all located in Nairobi and there are those for the High Court. These remandees are normally transported in a prison lorry under tight security by prison warders.

Those going for medication at Kenyatta National Hospital (KNH) and other clinics in the city of Nairobi are dispatched in similar prison lorries. The remandees, or prisoners, normally transported in those lorries are packed to capacity irrespective of their sickness.

One shudders to think of what would happen in an accident - the causality figure would be very high, assuming there would be survivors.

For those not going to court or hospitals, life goes on in a humdrum way. At about 9:00 a.m., the new entrants (remandees or prisoners) are called out for registration.

For 'prison language', registration means getting the prison number; your file is opened for you which contains details of yourself: like who will visit you, how you can make your correspondence – maybe to your bankers, institution(s) (read: where you were working or going to school etc.). The exercise is meant to give you an opportunity to get in touch with the people in an effort to put your records straight or in order, for you are not going to be a free person for a period, depending on your sentence.

Soon after the registration exercise, the sick persons are called out to be escorted to the prison dispensary for medical attention. Those not called out are of course locked in their block.

In most, if not all cases, a lot of prisoners or remandees fake illness and are allowed to go to the prison health centre or dispensary. They take the opportunity to go out and sun themselves under the guise of going for medical attention. The clinic is an important institution in the life of a remandee or prisoner. It could literally mean the difference between life and death.

The clinic, like in the case of Kamiti and Kodiaga, is manned by at least three to five Clinical Officers (COs) and nurses, while there is a doctor in charge. Always there are at least two to three warders to assist the medical staff in making sure that the sick prisoners or remandees are in an orderly manner, while waiting to be attended. The interesting aspect is that the medical personnel 'dish' out mainly aspirin liberally for all manner of ailments ranging from scabies, headache, coughing, malaria and even ulcer victims.

The only ailments which are treated differently are tuberculosis (TB) and diarrhea, which are quite common in prisons and remands. Another popular medicine, apart from aspirin, is piriton, which in fact helps the prisoners or remandees to have long spells of sleep.

In prison, to get to see the doctor or go to the clinic is not all that easy, you have first of all to get permission of the warders on duty and they have the in-charge, who will be consulted first before the prisoner/remandee is allowed. Getting permission alone may take two or three days. It can be same day only if the warders assess you physically and determine that you are obviously unwell, otherwise it takes one time to consider giving a prisoner or remandee permission to go out (of course on escort) for medical attention.

Equally, it is problematic to get a referral to outside hospitals or clinics. The prison doctor must get a lot of persuading unless you are on your last moments – facing death and even then you may have to talk to them (doctors) or clinical officers 'nicely' for them to refer you to an outside clinic or any other hospital outside prison. Talking 'nicely' in the prison language means bribing.

Some prisoners connive with prison warders or doctors to go outside for treatment. But, all is meant for them to meet relatives if not friends for certain gains. The prisoner/remandee in these circumstances must soften the warders and doctors for them to release him. This in itself is a great opportunity. There are cases when some prisoners fake sickness in order to be referred to an outside hospital, and yet it is an opportunity for transacting personal deals, especially 'big time prisoners'.

Prisoners Get Ready For Lunch at 11.00 AM

By about 11:00 a.m., the prisoner is getting ready for lunch. This meal is usually preceded or punctuated by another 'hesabu'. All remandees and prisoners are confined to their blocks for counting, unless they are caught by the 'hesabu' at the food serving bay.

The lunch is none other than 'ugali' with sometimes salted white cabbage or *sukuma wiki*. In fact, you will find a few leaves of greens, while there is a lot of water, which is literally salted and this does very well when it comes to eating 'prison ugali'.

Ordinarily this is the most dismal of meals, although at times the big brass are to be seen gloating, watching their 'charges' being fed on this 'sumptuous' meal. The charges are those prisoners who have been in prison for over five years and have long sentences of let's say 10, 15, 20 years to serve.

This means that they are trusted by the prison authorities and are assigned some responsibilities. They are kind of assistants to the prison warders. After the meals, all prisoners and remandees are locked up again unless a particular senior prison warder like a sergeant normally referred to or respectably called 'senior' is around. He is known to allow an hour or so for remandees to sun themselves or air their lice-ridden bedding(s).

Come 3:00 p.m., supper would normally be ready to be served! This meal is invariably ugali with beans. Fine, it is beans but its stew is three quarters of the mug. Prisoners find that stew more valuable than the beans.

The stew with few (countable) beans, is of boiled beans, least one be misled to think that the government is prepared to waste precious fat on remandees or prisoners. Beef stew is only served for the sick and those privileged to own a medical recommendation for special diet or are otherwise 'monied'.

Remandees and prisoners are served with one big piece of meat three days out of seven. On meat days, a lot of fanfare and vigorous 'barter trade' like business takes place. For example, the small piece of meat being exchanged for a cigarette. It is not only for prisoners or remandees, but equally the low ranked warders get vigorously involved in the business of 'barter trade'.

They (those involved) buy cigarettes to exchange with pieces of meat. In fact, it is a field day for prisoners and prison warders during meat eating days. The families of warders also enjoy for they will eat meat.

At least by 6:00 p.m. all remandees have been fed, save for those reporting late from either the courts or hospital from outside prison. In most cases the meal is over well before 7:00 p.m. The last lock-up takes place between 7:30 p.m. and 8:30 p.m., being earlier over the weekends and public holidays.

The prisoners/remandees are then left cooped up in their blocks. No movement being allowed up and the keys remitted to the offices of senior warders for safe keeping till the following day.

A typical block in the prison (Kamiti or Kodiaga for example) will have an average of 200 to 400 prisoners or roughly 900 in total. Each block is equipped with one or two toilets and a pipe which gushes water 24 hours a day. At times, some blocks have no water running, while a few have windows placed about 12 to 15 feet from the ground.

On a hot day, this turns to be an oven with very stale air. No wonder many remandees or prisoners succumb to Tuberculosis (TB) and other respiratory diseases.

The sleeping space is of course at a premium. It even turns out that on some nights, it is impossible to fit in all the occupants.

All Suspects Pleaded Guilty

In the mid-eighties whenever I read of the arrest and imprisonment of the alleged Mwakenya suspects and political dissidents, I would say: *"How can somebody just plead guilty and allow himself to go to prison without the services of a lawyer?"* or *"What is wrong with these dissidents who claim to be patriots that they dare not appeal against conviction and sentence?"*

All these questions and many others disturbed me, especially when I read of professionals going to prison by just pleading guilty in court to all that they were accused of. In fact, it affected men of various professions, for example, lawyers, journalists, medics and academicians among other professionals.

I wondered what kind of people they were (dissidents and Mwakenya suspects), that they would admit being guilty as soon as they are brought before a magistrate!

The other aspect I equally questioned, was why they were being taken to court for trial after 4:30 p.m. in all cases. In fact, no Mwakenya suspect or any 'dissident', related to the so-called underground or clandestine movements, was taken to court earlier than 4:30 p.m. Another aspect was that all suspects related to similar cases [read sedition] were tried in Nairobi before specific magistrates; many times before H.H. Buch who was a Chief Magistrate, while the Chief Prosecutor was none other than the then notorious Assistant Director of Public Prosecution [ADPP], Bernard Chunga. Chunga later became the Deputy Director of Public Prosecution [DDPP].

Chunga: Chief Prosecutor of,
"Mwakenya" related cases

He was rewarded to become Kenya's Chief Justice in late 1999 to replace the then late Chief Justice Zacheaus Chesoni.

In fact, come January 29, 1987, in the evening (shortly after 4:45 p.m.), I got the appropriate answers to the questions and the concerns that I have raised a while ago; which used to bother me whenever I read in the media about cases involving the so-called Mwakenya dissidents or perpetrators as they were referred to by the government's agents.

I got the answers to those questions a little later when I was arrested. Like other Mwakenya suspects, I was taken to court and made to plead guilty to a charge related to alleged Mwakenya activities and programmes.

I pleaded guilty to those charges after spending 45 days – one month and fifteen days at the Nyayo House Police Station's torture chambers, cells/dungeons, where like most of the Mwakenya suspects, I was held incommunicado and tortured to a point of despair.

Late Journalist Wahome, like his
brother Njuguna Mutahi of PAT was
jailed for 15 months

For the case of the late Wahome, a similar jail term of 15 months was handed down to his brother, Mr. Njuguna Mutahi, then a Kenya News Agency reporter. Mr. Njuguna was then based at Iten District Headquarters in Rift Valley, where he was an Information Officer.

Together that evening of January 28, 1987, I and the late Kamangara, were whisked in security vehicles under tight security escort to Kamiti Maximum Security Prison to start serving our sentences for offences that we had been induced to admit or confess to having committed.

If I can quote a fellow journalist, the late celebrated playwright Wahome Mutahi: *"A prison sentence looked a better prospect than a day longer at the Nyayo House torture chambers."* And I do concur with him.

Benard Chunga-Led Prosecutions

The after 4:30 p.m. stage-managed Mwakenya trials and similar or related cases were nothing but a mockery of the country's judicial system. The prosecution was led by none other than the former Chief Justice Bernard Chunga, whose education and academic background still remain a mystery and not clearly known to Kenyans to date.

Chunga, in fact, did his best as a government agent to paint us (Mwakenya suspects) with the heinous crime of sedition.

I had a number of questions and I tried to raise some of them, although I was not spared time and only managed to put some across to him I recall asking him, *"Mr. Chunga does it not occur in your mind that I have been brought to court after official working hours? And that I need legal representation?"* Also, *"Is your mind not guilty that this court is full of Special Branch police officers who have tortured me at Nyayo House torture chambers for over one month?"*

I further asked Chunga a series of questions, although I was restrained by the presiding Magistrate. *"Does it not concern you that there are no members of the public in this court? Don't you get concerned when you go about your daily life that trials against the alleged Mwakenya suspects are illegal for none is ever represented whenever you conduct your prosecutions?"*

"Mr. Chunga, if I showed you and the Magistrate my legs, you would be shocked. They are actually rotten because of being put in salted water for long hours during the torture sessions at Nyayo House torture chambers."

Efforts to raise these fundamental questions in the court, which was mainly packed with suspicious looking Special Branch police officers, were thwarted by Chunga with the assistance of the notorious Chief magistrate, H.H. Buch.

However, this would have been an opportunity for Chunga to ponder over the answers to the questions if I had been accorded a chance to raise them during the stage-managed Mwakenya trial.

I was, in fact, not allowed to ask prosecutor Chunga those questions since Mwakenya suspects were not allowed nor had any right to do so in the court.

One interesting aspect which may not be known to the public was that a Mwakenya suspect was only taken to court on condition that he had entered an MOU (Memorandum of Understanding) that he would plead guilty to the offence he was suspected of having committed. One or two changed their minds on arrival in court, pleaded not guilty, and were quickly whisked away by the dreaded 'James Opiyo torture boys' to Nyayo House only to be produced in court the following day or two days later, after their MOUs having been revised. This time around, the Opiyo boys ensured that their client entered a plea of being guilty. The questions raised here are: Why did the suspect plead guilty after one day or so? Why did the suspect change his mind to admit the offence that he had denied he committed?

January 29, 1987 Was a Dark Day

January 29, 1987, shall remain the darkest day in my life. It was a trial day in a Nairobi Court presided over by Chief Magistrate, H.H. Buch and the prosecutor was Bernard Chunga.

On arrival at the Nairobi Law Court, I found that I was in the company of one Nakuru politician – John Maina Kamangara. I was taken to the court shortly after 4:45 p.m., while blindfolded and bundled into the back seat of a white, unmarked, short chassis Land Rover.

I was told by one of my top interrogators a Mr. Francis Ndirangu:

"You are now going to be legally and procedurally released through the court, for you have been with us assisting in the investigations in connection with Mwakenya activities and its program. All we want to avoid is for you and your relatives not to sue the government for arresting and confining you for more than the legally stipulated period."

"You know well that you were held 'incommunicado'. You are a journalist, and therefore an informed Kenyan citizen. Don't have any fears, you will be released, but all the same you will have to be taken to the court and be released there."

The interrogator who was very friendly further pleaded with me not to be 'uncooperative' with the Magistrate and the prosecutor when I appeared before them.

At 5:35 p.m., while at the dock I spotted my wife Margaret, my elder brother Nicholas (Achira) and my other brother David (Onyancha), the lawyer, my late father (Mzee Joseph Achira) and a few other relatives and a handful of friends. They were anxious from the look of their faces and body language.

Even while still at the dock, the interrogator came next to me and whispered, *"Mr. Achira you just cooperate as agreed earlier and the prosecutor Chunga will give his side of the story and the Magistrate shall formally make some remarks to the effect that you have cooperated with the investigators and being remorseful you have been formally released."*

My interrogator went further to convince me that they (investigators) made it possible for my relatives to be in court and shall pay the fine that was to be imposed on me!

"They (read: relatives) were informed to come and collect you upon your release today."

I, at this point, told the interrogator, *"I know you are cheating me. All you want is to have me plead guilty and send me to prison. I will certainly do it for prison is a better option than where I have been for the past 45 days since I was arrested."*

The interrogator was left with no words, for I was already in the dock waiting for the presiding magistrate and the prosecutor to emerge from their offices to the court room. He tried to console himself and comfort me by saying, *"You will certainly be released today"*

The presiding Magistrate emerged from his office, while the prosecutor also appeared from the next door just next to me. At this stage I heard the court clerk call my names. *"James Omwega Achira, you are accused of being a member of a clandestine movement known as Mwakenya."* I never responded but looked at the Chief Magistrate, the prosecutor and two of my interrogators, Chief Inspector Jacob Katama whispered to me - *"You admit and you will be released as agreed."*

"You are a liar and you have all conspired to have me jailed!" I shouted at the Inspector, who shied off as some of my relatives and Special Branch police officers looked at me with dismay.

The court clerk, as if obliging to my outburst, addressed the court, which was packed with security agents of the state and a handful of my relatives plus court officers, *"That being a member of unlawful Society Contrary to Section 6(a) of the Societies Act Cap 108 Laws of Kenya, between October 1981 and December 15, 1986 at Nairobi within Nairobi area you were a member of an unlawful society known as Mwakenya, knowing and having reasonable cause to believe that the said Mwakenya was an unlawful society."*

I was charged and cautioned by one Chief Inspector Jacob Katama of Criminal Investigations Department (CID) unit within the Police Force. CIP Katama apparently who was from the CID Headquarters was attached to Nairobi area.

CIP Katama charged and cautioned me at 2:32 p.m. on

January 26, 1987 at Nyayo House Police Station on the 25th floor, but I was taken to court late in the evening on January 29, 1987

I was informed that I would be taken to court on the same day if I agreed to plead guilty. On January 26 1987 my clothes were wet and this may have caused the Opiyo boys to not take me to court until the next day, January 29, 1987.

After prosecutor Chunga's presentation of the so-called 'facts' of the case which lasted for close to 20 minutes, I was also asked to mitigate before the ruling or the verdict of the Chief Magistrate. My mitigation lasted for ten minutes.

In fact, it is important to take note that my mitigating facts had been prepared by my interrogators and handed over to me. They told me that if I used those facts the magistrate will certainly release me. I knew this was not true but accepted it to escape the torture chambers and go to prison instead.

Prosecutor Chunga in his presentation had this to state. *"The accused is a journalist by profession and has been in the practice here in Nairobi and many other parts of the country including Kisii, South Nyanza, Kisumu and Nakuru. He is a scholar and therefore a man of no mean intelligence, who knows his rights. He interacts and relates with all kinds of personalities. He is very well known and he well knew that the clandestine movement was dangerous and its members were a security risk to the country's welfare and he willingly joined the movement and actively participated in its activities and programmes which he knew were detrimental to the State Security."*

"The accused," Chunga stated, *"Met and dined with leading dissidents in this country in the course of which they planned and agreed on how to perpetuate the Mwakenya activities in order to cause instability and this meant to subsequently undermine the good government of this country*

under the wise leadership of his Excellency President Daniel Arap Moi".

"For the accused to desist in future from similar and other related activities, I call upon this honourable court to issue a deterrent sentence to the accused to serve as a lesson to others who have not been to this court."

Chunga further added: *"It will not be enough for the accused to be warned and be released or be fined but, a custodial sentence is necessary for these activities were detrimental and destructive to the welfare of peace loving Kenyans and the general state security was threatened by his activities."*

Chunga continued in his submission: *"Taking into account the interrogation and confession, the accused had been sponsored to go to Arusha in Tanzania in the pretext of pursuing further studies while he was there to conduct some recruitment of Kenyan 'dissidents', who were based in Tanzania and mainly in Arusha, Mwanza and Dar es Salaam. I urge this honourable court to consider the fact and the seriousness of the activities of the accused and hand down a deterrent sentence to serve as an example to his colleagues."*

After Chunga's submission, in which he vigorously urged the court (Chief Magistrate H.H. Buch) to issue a deterrent sentence. I was given an opportunity to mitigate.

In fact, before I was charged and cautioned, two of my interrogators offered to write down for me the mitigating factors. I accepted, for I knew well that was the trick for me to ease their work and clear me from Nyayo House Police Station dungeons/cells and the torture chambers. I was convinced that I was headed for either prison or detention after one month and 15 days of stay at the Nyayo House basement.

Mitigation after Chunga's Submission

"Your honour, I am married with two children aged between six years and one year. The two children, your

honour, need my presence and that fatherly advice, love and care for them to grow up and become upright citizens of our country.

"Your honour, since my marriage is still young - six years old, my wife needs my presence, comfort and guidance for we need to nurture and bring up a stable and upright family which will also have a role to play in the nation building of this country.

"Your honour, I am the second born in a family of 11 children and my parents who are small-scale farmers in Nyamira are looking forward to getting my support upon completion of my higher studies, and my sisters and brothers are still in school and they need the financial support of which I was a contributor. Your honour, at the time of my arrest on December 15, 1986, in Kisii Town, I had just arrived eight days ago from Mwanza, Tanzania for my December vacation from college, where I was undertaking a two-year diploma course in Journalism Studies.

"At the time of my arrest," I continued. "I had just completed one academic year of the course and I was to start the first semester of my second year on January 5th, this year (1987). I have sponsored myself for the two-year programme. I pay a substantial sum of money, of which if jailed, will be a great loss to me and my family.

"Your honour, last year alone, I paid Kenya shillings 116,000 in tuition fees including personal expenses, and this year I shall pay a similar amount. Your honour all personal valuables and effects – academic certificates, professional tools are at the college, which is located 18 kilometers south of Mwanza Town on the shores of Lake Victoria and over 700 kilometers away from here.

"Your honour, at the College, I am the Secretary General of the Foreign Students Body; an organization which takes care of their interests and welfare. Those foreign students, your honour, come from various Eastern, Central and West African countries. Your honour, as we closed College for

December vacation, I had in my custody very vital documents of about 24 foreign students at college which included resident permits, passports and other related documents that were assisting in processing their resident permits. I was working in collaboration with the dean of students to process their resident permits, while the old ones were due for renewal for this year.

"Your honour, in my life time, now about 30 years to be precise, since I became a public figure I have been loyal, honest, patriotic and truthful to my government, country and the ruling party – KANU. I have never committed any crime or offence nor have I had intentions to commit an offence. I have never offended the state, if any, maybe this is my first offence. I have total confidence in the leadership of our President.

"Your honour, since I was arrested on December 15, 1986 it is today (January 29, 1987) one month and 15 days, and while in police custody I have suffered a lot and in the process I have learnt a lesson: as a citizen of this country I have a duty and responsibility to defend and protect my country at all times whether within or outside the country.

"Your honour, I promise here today that I shall always remain patriotic to my country despite all the intimidation, torture -- both mental and physical together with psychological suffering I underwent during the 45 days in the hands of the state agents, in confinement at various police stations and eventually at the Nyayo House Police Station.

"Your honour, the offence which has brought me before the court today I had committed it by being misled by a friend. I joined an illegal movement and I am very sorry about it. I am equally remorseful. I shall always guard myself from the activities of the movement if released today.

"In addition, your honour, I appeal to those who have ill-feelings about our good government and are currently engaged in illegal and subversive activities against our legal *and constitutional government to stop and become good and patriotic citizens.*

"In conclusion, your honour, I pray and beg the court to have mercy on me and exercise leniency so as to give me a non-custodial sentence. In view of the above factors a non-custodial sentence shall enable me to proceed with my studies and be with my young family. That is all, your honour."

In fact, as I started my mitigation, the interrogators, state security agents in the court room, prosecutor Chunga, H.H. Buch and other court officers listened with a lot of interest, while prosecutor Chunga as well as Chief Inspector Katama (CIP Katama charged and cautioned me on January 26, 1987 at 2:32 p.m.) were staring at me and their body language was telling. At some stage, prosecutor Chunga intervened and begged H.H. Buch to stop me from telling the court a story, but the magistrate said: *"Proceed, please and don't repeat yourself."*

Another interesting aspect was that the court officers and state security agents seemed to be following my mitigating factors with a lot of interest. At one stage when I stated that *"I shall remain patriotic to my country at all times of my life in spite of all the intimidation and torture I underwent during my confinement at various police stations......"* their faces changed as some of them looked at me very keenly and with intimidating faces. But, this did not scare me, for I was, in fact, convinced that I was headed for either detention or prison. But, in the back of my mind, I convinced myself that I was prison material. If it was detention, there was no reason why I was brought before H.H. Buch. For detention, an order was to be signed by the Minister of State and Internal Security, after which I was to be served and driven to a detention camp, without going through the court.

At the end of my mitigation, my suspicion became true. Indeed, I was convicted and sentenced to 24 months and consigned to Kamiti Maximum Security Prison, Nairobi.

However, before conviction and sentence, when the security agents and my interrogators heard me say *"I had committed the offence because I was misled by a friend in joining the illegal movement and I am very sorry about it ..."* Their faces, especially the two who were my interrogators (Wachira and Ndirangu), CIP Katama and that of the then notorious state prosecutor Chunga, shined. This actually for them was a big score and meant that they were on their way to success.

Upon completing mitigation, the late H.H. Buch looked at me and coughed. All my relatives were holding their breath, while the state agents wore smiling faces as the entire court room remained unusually silent.

H.H. Buch had this to say; *"After listening to the prosecutor's submission and keenly sieving the facts which led to the arrest of the accused before me. I have learnt and adduced one important aspect – the accused Mr. Achira is a scholar, Kenyan citizen who knew and still knows his role in society. He should have guarded himself against being recruited hence being misled to joining an illegal movement. I have also listened to the accused's mitigating factors and I sympathise with his predicament, but he has to go to prison for two years for his illegal activities in the clandestine movement, Mwakenya, to serve as an example to the rest who are involved or intend to involve themselves in such illegal activities that are detrimental to the state security."*

At this point, I could not believe my ears. I saw the state security agents and other court officers stand up and move to a corner whispering to one another, while my relatives (among them my wife and my brothers) moved closer to me to give a word or so of consolation.

Reporter Andrew Kuria of *Daily Nation* and Nation's Chief Photographer, Mohamed came closer to me. Kuria told me, *"Jimmy, take heart. You are fortunate that your sentence is extremely light. Others received four, five, even six years. The previous day (January 28, 1987) the same court handed down between four and six years to some people accused of being involved in Mwakenya activities."*

Kuria, a renowned court reporter then, told me that of the 24 months (two years), I shall only be in prison for less than 18 months. And indeed, my sentence ended up being 15 months, not 24 months! I was convicted and jailed on January 29, 1987 and released on May 29, 1988.

After a word of consolation from reporter Kuria and the photographer Mohamed, other colleagues from the media and my relatives, I was led out of the court room to the court's basement while photographers jostled for my picture; and indeed they got it.

My wife could not hold back her tears, while my brothers braved it and followed me to the basement. All they did was to comfort me and said words of encouragement before they left. It was approaching 7:00 p.m. I, at this point, was in a state of confusion. I did not know what was next or what to do. But all that was waiting for me was to start my two-year sentence at Kamiti Maximum Security Prison, Nairobi.

At about 7:10 p.m., I and Mr. Kamangara were in the hands of the prison warders. The interrogators (James Opiyo's boys) were nowhere to be seen. Their mission well executed, we were put in a prison van and started a journey that ended up at Kamiti Prison. I had not been to court before, nor had I been to prison even as a visitor.

On arrival at Kamiti, we found that prisoners had been locked up in their rooms, except a few who were going about certain essential services like assisting the warders. In addition to the two Mwakenya convicts (the author and Kamangara), there were three other persons.

Arriving after 7:15 p.m. meant that supper was over. However, the warders, when told that we were 'political prisoners', got excited and from nowhere prisoners nicknamed 'trustees' were summoned and were told that they must ensure that we have been served with food.

After about ten minutes, ugali and maharagwe together with some two or so pieces of meat were given to us.

Prison warders and remandees were curious to know who we were and what offence(s) we had committed. I got to know that the name Kamangara was a household name at Kamiti Prison then. The warder and the 'trustees' got excited and started chatting with Kamangara, who in fact was not shocked like myself that I was in prison. I later on learnt that Kamangara had been to Kamiti (as a guest of the Kenya government) a few months back.

After our 'supper', which I never ate, we were taken to a cell in the segregation block where we were given two old, torn blankets each, and dirty prison uniforms known in the prison jargon as "Kunguru."

At segregation block, I was given instructions and a stern warning not to talk to anybody of what brought me to prison. I was put in a cell alone. I had two old blankets and there was nothing in the cell I was locked in. The lighting was extremely dim and the walls of the cell were dark-grey.

My colleague Kamangara was locked in a separate cell, and I overheard a prison warder caution him not to talk to anybody about why he was imprisoned. The warders who took us to the cells, which were adjacent to each other, informed us that they shall come for us the following morning for other formalities that we did not complete when we arrived at Kamiti Maximum Prison.

The following day – January 30, 1987 the day started as usual in a prison and we (Kamangara and I) were escorted by prison warders to an officer. We were received by an officer of the rank of Chief Inspector of Police. In prison terminology, the officer was Chief Officer One (COI).

The office we were in was known as Documentation Office (DO). I was issued with a prison card bearing the offence committed, duration of incarceration and the EPD – the jail term less remission of a third (1/3) of the sentence.

Technically therefore, I was meant to serve 18 months and not 24 months (two years); if in the opinion of the prison authorities, I remained of good conduct and behaviour while serving my jail term.

Always, the prison warders who were assigned to guard me and others – so labeled as 'political prisoners' were people who were trained or had instructions not to talk to us. Our occasional chats were only about the weather. In prison, it was another torture just to sit staring at the four walls and the sky. Actually, the walls were more than nine feet high.

Contrary to what many believe, manual work in prison is actually appreciated by prisoners. This is because, if you get to do some manual work or something involving physical exercise the better, because by the time you get to bed after such work, you easily fall asleep. This is because in prison, one really longs for sleep.

In prison, Sundays are the best days for prisoners, since inmates are allowed to go to church and so they get to meet and interact with one another, although it was very much regulated for prisoners of our category – 'political prisoners'.

It is in the church that I received notes from fellow inmates which informed me what they were going through. Their experiences were difficult to believe, but otherwise true. It was also in the church when we were about to go in for the service to start, and when it was over, at least we had five to ten minutes chat, which was a lot. One gets to know what the goings-on within and outside prison are. Many prisoners long for Sundays.

The first visitor who came to see me the following day (after I was convicted and sentenced on January 29, 1987) was my brother, the lawyer, Mr. David Nyakang'o Onyancha.

At the visitors' room of Kamiti Maximum Security Prison's main gate we had a chat over the possibilities of an appeal against conviction and sentence or against the sentence alone.

I felt the sharing or discussion with my brother was not flowing or was not consistent. We resolved that I be left to rest and settle down for a week or so, while I ponder over the possibility of whether to appeal or not.

The second visitor was a friend of mine – one Bob Mogusu, a businessman then based at Kamiti Shopping Centre. Bob had come to see me upon reading the Friday *Nation* of January 30, 1987 that I had been convicted and sentenced to two years in prison.

He wondered how, for he knew I was away at college. Bob, it turned out later was to be the father-in-law to my brother, the lawyer. My brother's wife, Esther Kerubo, is the niece to Bob Mogusu. Bob came to visit me at Kamiti Prison on the basis that he was a good friend. We had known one another before I got to know that his niece was going to be my brother's wife. Bob consoled me in the officer's office at the main gate of the prison. Maybe he talked to prison officers, who from time to time had a soft heart on me for the period I was at Kamiti, before I was moved to Kisumu (Kodiaga Main Prison) after a period of about six months.

Life in prison was like a puzzle having to wake up at 5:00 a.m. every day except weekends, public holidays or national days like Madaraka Day when wake up time is rescheduled to 6:00 a.m.

Every day after waking up, breakfast was white porridge. I was told that this would go on like this every morning until I completed my jail term of two years!

Every night, as I retired to 'Segregation Block' (dormitory), I shared with other 'political prisoners', a sense of hopelessness descended on me; the pain of going to sleep without knowing whether my children, my wife and my parents were with me in their hearts and prayers.

I had the will power to survive. I never broke down despite the disturbing developments. I knew that somehow I would get out of incarceration and see my children, wife, parents, relatives and friends. I also knew that my family was helpless in the face of the judgement – for it was dirty politics which were at play. I knew that somehow, I would get out of it in the end. All I did was look forward to the day I would tell my story.

My parents, sisters and brothers gave my wife and children (Wycliffe and Douglas) all the comfort. My brother – the lawyer -- had to work extra hard to ensure that he assisted my wife and my children, although my wife had a job with Agricultural Finance Corporation (AFC).

That is not to say that other relatives did not play any role – Sammy Omwega Ondari, my cousin and age-mate, who had been to prison himself, had consoled my family by giving them courage and hope. That kept them going until it was May 29, 1988 – the day I was released from prison at Kisumu's Kodiaga Prison.

My cousin had not committed any criminal offence that warranted him to go to prison. It was as a result of the attempted coup of August 1, 1982, staged by the Kenya Air Force (KAF), in which my cousin was enlisted.

Sammy was an officer with KAF, and the weekend the coup attempt took place, he was on leave. He had arrived from Britain where he had been for some course sponsored by the military. The charge against him (Sammy Omwega Ondari) was that he failed to report the coup.

Although I was worried about those close to my heart, I never gave up one thing; I trusted in God and prayed every day. I convinced myself that appealing against conviction and sentence may not be of much value. The reason being, it was the state which planned and executed the entire stage-managed arrest, confinement, torture and court trial.

At prison, my day began unlike other prisoners with breakfast. For me, and other prisoners who were jailed under similar circumstances, I was not supposed to join other prisoners for any manual work. We would be confined to our rooms normally classified as 'segregation block'. In prison, lunch was served at 11:30 a.m. and work resumed at 12:30 p.m. until 5:30 p.m. when supper was served. But for me and other political prisoners, we would only drink, eat and get locked up in our rooms.

At the start of our jail terms, we were locked in rooms in ones. But later on in threes; this was so because as time went by the number of the so-called political prisoners increased. This was so because 1987 was the year that saw the Kenya government arrest Kenyan scholars, lawyers, journalists and other profesionals, which it branded as 'dissidents'. Also arrested and jailed then were university students especially student leaders.

Water was a rare commodity; and there were not enough toilets and bathrooms. Those which were available were ever congested (blocked). We seldom bathed because there was hardly any water flowing from the taps.

Like all other prisoners, I slept on the floor, although with at least two blankets – one to spread and other to cover myself. But one thing I did appreciate is that the prison warders were kind, polite and supportive in many ways. The warders were supportive because I was a 'political prisoner' and they (warders) knew we were set to take over the government led by Moi, and that we would have been their 'saviours.' Reason being, prison warders led very humiliating lives. They were poorly paid and poorly housed; and this they attributed to the government of the day. Therefore, anything they would hear of or told that was close to getting a better government was their menu.

It is on that basis – poor housing, poor pay, poor clothing, that prisoner warders were good friends of the so-called political prisoners. All those who were convicted and jailed as a result of illegal movements – December Twelve Movement, Mwakenya and other related cases that touch on treason or sedition received, in most cases, heroic treatment in Kenyan prisons!

April 10, 2003, Daily Nation

Motion on payment of torture victims passed

Parliament yesterday passed a motion seeking compensation for victims of torture and detention, but with amendments.

The government watered down the private member's motion, by Mr Koigi Wamwere (Subukia, Nare), before throwing its weight behind it. Those to be compensated include former MPs and university dons.

Office of the President assistant minister Stephen Tarus said the amendment was seeking the formation of a House committee to collect views from former MPs, academics and other Kenyans who were either tortured or were detained by the past regime forcing some of them to flee the country.

The committee would then table its recommendations to the House.

Among the most famous ex-detainees are Saba Saba Asili leader Kenneth Matiba, and former minister Charles Rubia, Public Works minister Raila Odinga and former MPs Martin Shikuku and George Anyona.

Admitting that many people had suffered in torture chambers and detention camps since independence, Mr Tarus requested the mover of the motion to accept his amendments.

He was supported by Finance assistant minister Mutua Katuku who said many people had suffered under Kanu and it was time to come together as a

Clashed over abuses

Mr Wamwere   Mr Kariuki

Earlier, Mr Wamwere and another former detainee clashed with former internal security minister G.G. Kariuki (Laikipia West, Narc) over his role in the torture and detention of government critics in the 1980s.

Mr Wamwere and Mr Mirugi Kariuki (Nakuru Town, Narc) took Mr Kariuki to task for opposing the motion.

For the second time in a week, the Laikipia West MP rose to defend himself against claims by his critics that he was involved in the excesses of the previous regime as internal security minister.

Rising on a point of order, Mr Kariuki said: "It is true what Koigi has said that I opposed the motion, but it was before the government came in and asked for an amendment."

Added the Laikipia East MP: "Is he suggesting that I was in charge when ...

left government in 1983 while these things took place thereafter. Could he read my book, *Illusion of Power*, to set the record straight."

The Nakuru Town MP said no amount of compensation would cover for the mental, physical and psychological torture the victims went through.

"What we are asking for is just a token by the government as a sign of apology," he said adding, "We know the architects of the past regime are still with us in his House, such as GG."

It was at that point that the Laikipia West MP shot up and defended himself.

Replying to members contributions to his motion, Mr Wamwere thanked the government for supporting it with amendments.

The Subukia MP said all he was seeking was "medicine to help cure the victims of past human rights abuses".

Mr Wamwere reminded members that the governing party had pledged to compensate victims of torture during its campaigns.

The motion was also supported by Dr Ali Wario (Bura, Kanu), Mr Gonzi Rai (Kinango, Ford People) and Dr Bonny Khalwale (Ikolomani, Narc) who said time had come for the country to come to terms with its past as it looks into the future.

Dr Khalwale said some of the victims were castrated and called on the government to compensate them.

85

PART TWO

AFTER OPENING OF TORTURE CHAMBERS

In part II, the author discusses various issues based on the opening of "Nyayo House Police Station", which led to the opening of Nyayo House torture chambers, cells and dungeons; then he wondered loudly: What on earth were the torture chambers at Nyayo House for?

Following the opening of torture chambers on February 11, 2003, the Nyayo House victims/ survivors met the (then) Minister for Justice and Constitutional Affairs, Mr. Kiraitu Murungi, and made the following statement (a memorandum) below – (Make Torture Chambers Public Museum). It was read by Journalist Njuguna Mutahi, Chair, The People Against Torture (PAT), who was himself a victim and was a 'guest' of Moi-KANU government at Kamiti Maximum Security camp for 15 months, like his late brother, the playwright/writer, Wahome Mutahi.

Make Torture Chambers Public Museum

We survivors of the Nyayo House torture chambers are assembled here today (February 11, 2003) to get a commitment from the NARC government that torture issues past and present shall be addressed adequately. Our visit to inspect the torture chambers is therefore symbolic. We are specifically requesting that the government:

- Conduct independent and thorough investigations into incidents of torture during the rule of the former government and institute measures to redress the same.
- Revoke Legal Notice No. 11 of February 1, 1991 declaring Nyayo House torture chambers as a protected area.

- Prioritize the passing of the amended Evidence Act to make confessions made to police officers inadmissible as evidence in court.
- Ensure immediate prosecution of all persons involved in torture and specifically former Assistant Commissioner of Police, James Opiyo, and the team that was in charge of the Nyayo torture chambers.
- Put in place the structure and mechanism for compensation of all torture victims.
- Convert Nyayo House torture chambers into national museums open to the public.
- Domesticate the Convention Against Torture (CAT), which it ratified on February 11, 1997 to enable Kenyans to use the convention in Kenya courts.
- Ratify the Rome Statute of the International Criminal Court so that people suspected of war crimes, genocide or crimes against humanity in Kenya are liable for prosecution at the court.
- Ratify the Second Optional Protocol to the United Nation's Convention Civil and Political Rights as testament of its commitment to guaranteeing the right to life of all citizens.

What on earth were the torture chambers for at the "Nyayo House Police Station?" Who built them and why?

Torture Chambers: An After Thought?

There is some consensus that the torture under Moi-KANU era represented an overreaction and excessive force to the threats that were at best minimal.

There is also the feeling that the torture was planned as part and parcel of the Moi-KANU regime and never came as an afterthought. Nyayo House came up in the late 1980s, complete with torture chambers, cells and dungeons; an indication that rule by terror was on the way.

A. A. Ngotho, the Chief Government Architect, says

when Nyayo House was built; it was put up for the Special Branch Police. His department (read: Ngotho's) dealt strictly with three people at the Special Branch's directorate.

The three were two senior officials of the Directorate of Special Branch and a Mr. Parkins, a British national, whose role in Special Branch Directorate, Ngotho never knew.

Ngotho recalls that Parkins would come and change the plan of the building at will from time to time but never said what the changes in the building were for.

During, the construction of the building, the Special Branch had its team of technicians who did the electrical fittings and fixed the telephone system, Ngotho recalls.

"The threat to Moi-KANU regime was imaginary. Moi embraced torture to pacify the kind of opposition that was mounting and went ahead to ban multiparty democracy. There was no justification at all for the kind of force the regime used on us," Raila Odinga, then Cabinet Minister, was quoted by the local press while he visited the torture chambers on February 14, 2003, in the company of some torture victims including the author.

Raila Odinga: "Force used was not justified"

Interestingly, in what seems to have been borrowed from the Romanian torture chambers, the torturers would play for the prisoners/suspects tapes of babies and children screaming, crying etc.

They would tell prisoners that those were voices of their children.

The prisoners would be told that they were hearing their own sons and daughters being slowly tortured and that the children would be killed if they (prisoners) did not cooperate and confess to the alleged claims and allegations by their torturers.

Torture Chambers at a Glance

A man who was detained in Nyayo House torture chambers for 24 days (and later convicted of sedition and jailed for 14 months), had this to tell but asked for anonymity.

"The chambers were at the 24th and 25th floors of Nyayo House building, Nairobi. But the dungeons and cells were at the basement of the building." The man (read: torture victim and survivor) decided to tell his experiences. In fact, his experiences were like a case study. However, there are individual experiences as told elsewhere in this book.

"As a victim of torture at the Nyayo House torture chambers and cells which are a replica of the death chambers, I wish to thank God that my colleagues and I left those cells alive.

"More than 20 years after leaving those torture chambers and cells, whose extensions are on floors 24 and 25 of Nyayo House, in Nairobi, the effects of torture linger in my mind. And did you know the government, in the *Kenya Gazette of February 1, 1991*, declared these chambers a restricted area? What a clever move to prevent wananchi, churchmen, lawyers or journalists from visiting the cells to find out where they 'teach suspects a lesson they cannot forget'.

"The leader of the torture squad was James Opiyo. I don't know whether this was his genuine or false name. But for those who have gone through the cells, that was a familiar name.

"If you have read accounts of Ugandan dictator Idi Amin's Secret Research Bureau (SRB) or the *Securitate* of Nicolae Ceausescu, former Romanian strongman, then you can picture how the Nyayo House squad operated. Do those Kenyan men know what happened to the SRB or *Securitate* agents when their masters fell?

"Torture cells at Nyayo House basement measure something like seven by seven feet, painted dull grey. But little of their original paint remains. It had been replaced by a thick layer of dirt and stains. Nobody washes these cells. Washing them would defeat the purpose for which they were meant: torture.

"They are generally dark but are dimly lit during tea or meal times, for a maximum of 15 minutes daily. Often you hear strange noises, like heavy footsteps of animals fighting in a small enclosure. You will never know what these noises really are unless Opiyo and his team tell us.

"The cells contain cold water, whose volume is controlled by Opiyo's men. When you are taken to a cell, you should expect to stand in the water, naked, for long periods. The water is at least ankle-high. For the first three to four days, you might not get food or water. How about if you want to answer nature's call? You have your cell. Do it there! The squad ensures you urinate and excrete in your cell. That is part of the torture, and if you are thirsty? Drink your urine or the contaminated water in your cell!

"If you think you are strong, you might try to fight off the temptation to drink this shit for one, two or three days. But what do you do on day four or five? Others might say you pray. But while you are there, you realize you have forgotten most of the prayers your priest had taught you when you were a child.

"At regular intervals, Opiyo's boys use a high pressure jet to pump very cold water into your cell. They target you. You want to escape. You curse because you are a man. You pretend not to cry. Your feet are beginning to rot. Your buttocks are swelling. The filth and the odour in your cell are becoming unbearable. For how long will this continue? You ask yourself if you are really going to live.

"Before they send you to court, Opiyo's boys will ensure you have been out of that goddamn cell for at least seven days. The court should never get the impression anyone tortured you. You should be walking straight not limping.

"But as days go by, you start dosing while you're standing; it is disgusting. You want to sleep; you can't. You want to sit; you can't. You want to stretch your legs; you can't. You feel pain all over your body. You think about your family. Do they know what you are being subjected to? Can you escape; no. You're at the mercy of your torturers.

"While you are in your cell, senior torturers will be sending their juniors to come and take you blindfolded upstairs to the 24th or 25th floor. Those seasoned torturers - senior police officers will be waiting to question you while you are naked. But that does not bother them.

"What are they up to? They want you to sign a false statement implicating yourself in the alleged crime. They will persuade you and one of them will say: 'Bwana, just sign here. You'll be free.' Or they will threaten to beat you up and the entire group will look at you with their firely eyes.

"Suddenly, they go wild, get their stakes and rungus and clobber you like a snake. They stop beating you for a while and ask if you are ready to sign the statement, to convict yourself. You sign the prepared statement and the beatings stop. You don't and the beating continues. You are returned to your basement cell. The entire exercise repeats itself until such time that you accept to sign a false statement, which shall be used to prosecute you."

Torture Chambers of Crime and Punishment

As Viewed By Prof. Egara Kabaji

"The opening of the Nyayo House torture chambers to the public made me reflect on the issue of crime and punishment. What came to my mind immediately is the experience of Fyodor Mikhaylovich Dostoyevsky, the Great Russian novelist and short story writer.

"On April 23, 1949, Fyodor M. Dostoyevsky and other members of the Petrashevsky spent eight months in prison until December 22, 1949 when the prisoners were led, without warning, to the Semyonovsky Square. In this square, a sentence of death by firing squad was pronounced, last rites were offered and three prisoners including Dostoyevsky were led out to be shot first.

"At the last possible moment, the guns were lowered and a messenger arrived with the information that the tsar had decided to spare their lives. The mock-execution ceremony was in fact part of the punishment. One of the prisoners went permanently insane on the spot while Dostoyevsky recovered to write the famous masterpieces, 'Crime and Punishment', and other books.

"Instead of being executed, Dostoyevsky was sentenced to four years in a Siberian prison labour camp to be followed by an indefinite term as a soldier. After his return to Russia, ten years later, he wrote a novel based on his prison camp experiences, 'The House of the Dead'. The novel describes the horrors that Dostoyesvky actually witnessed.

"'The House of the Dead' illustrates that more than anything else; it is the need for individual freedom that makes us human. Interestingly Dostoyevsky's description of Russian jails of 19th century does not match Kenya's 20th century Nyayo House torture chambers.

"Talk of development, and for sure we are ahead of the Russians of the 19th century. What I, however, delight in

is that we have so far, amassed a body of literary pieces that detail our inhumanity and which draw facts from Nyayo House monument of shame.

"Although extreme forms of punishment have been documented during the Nazi era, in independent Kenya the Nyayo House torture chambers should join those who sang praises of Nyayo era. Ngugi wa Thiong'o and others were lucky, for they were incarcerated at Kamiti Maximum Prison while the architect was still at work designing the Nyayo House torture chambers.

"Ngugi, nevertheless, records extreme forms of torture at Kamiti in his 'Detained - a Writer's Prison Dairy'. He writes: 'One of the most oppressive and offensive practices to human dignity were the chaining of detainees before giving them medical treatment or allowing them to see their wives and children.'

"Those who had the misfortune of being hospitalized received even worse treatment.

"Even in the operating theatre, their legs were chained to bed frames while armed police men and prison warders stood guard night and day. This, I think, is but a fraction of what transpired at Nyayo House chambers of torture.

"Ngugi's tribulations did not end with his release from detention. The University of Nairobi refused to reinstate him as professor of Literature. One senses the multiplier existed as the 'mother of all torture chambers', other small Nyayo houses are dotted all over the country in which progressive writers and artists were generally tormented. The latest to fall victim of the small Nyayo Houses is Prof. Kimani Njogu of Kiswahili Department of Kenyattta University.

"One is left wondering how and why a department of a university would want to torment, hound and lose a professor of world eminence with immense training paid for by the taxpayer. Prof. Francis Imbuga was tormented and frustrated; he had no option but to resign his job at Kenyatta

University. It is, I submit, the turning of public institutions into fiefdoms that breeds and nurtures the torturers and small Nyayo Houses.

"Well, it appears that in Ngugi's time in jail, the government had really not perfected torture techniques. Those who have read what we may call the Nyayo House inspired treatise will not only be shocked at the tendency of tortures to achieve a kind of organismic experience out of torture, but also learn that inside a human being, there is a primordial evil which, if ignited robs the individual of humanity, giving his animal instincts free reign.

"For many people, this evil was ignited in the 1980s. On a personal level, it was a shock to be informed that Robert Wafula Buke had been arrested. I happened to know Buke very well since our days at the National Youth Service (NYS.). I knew him as an avid reader of biographies and autobiographies of great people. We spent many hours discussing biographies of Martin Luther King and Mahatma Gandhi. I did not find him dangerous at all. Besides, Buke did not have a capacity to overthrow the government.

"In any case, to overthrow a government is not as easy as taking someone's girlfriend. Buke was to spend a number of months in Nyayo House torture chambers and later in prisons!

"But Buke is yet to give us his literary treatise. It was Wahome Mutahi, who fired perhaps the first fictional rendition of the Nyayo House experience in 'Three Days on the Cross' (1991).

"In this book, the late Wahome focuses on the brutality and inhumanity of Kenyans against other Kenyans. The writer's intention, it appears, was to arouse the conscience of those charged with the duty of maintaining law and order. The late Wahome does not really condemn the police who inflict pain but blames the system that produces them. The torturer's survival depends on their ability to show the 'illustrious one' that they are cracking down on dissidents.

"Wanyiri Kihoro's 'Never Say Die' relives 1,035 days in the hands of the Kenyan police. The setting is once again in the 1980s during the crackdown on the political dissent in Kenya. The overall message the author passes across, is that the crackdown resulted in gross violation of human rights. It was the innocent people who suffered in the Nyayo House torture chambers.

"The security men are insensitive to being grossly inhuman and insensitive to the rule of law. Their obsession with a desire to inflict pain should be the subject of study by psychologists.

"The disrespect to individual liberties reflects the working of a one party state in the Kenya of the 1980s. The book also reflects on a number of pertinent issues that should inform the government policies. It, for instance poses the question, 'have we lived up to the ideals set by our freedom/ independence fighters?'

"Why have we been unable to furnish ourselves with certain values and standards, which would help us judge our actions and experiences? Why are we unable to tolerate dissenting views? Why do we swerve from a certain minimum standard of decency and fair play? These questions could not be addressed by the previous regime – Moi-KANU government.

"Late Prof. Katama Mkangi's 'Walenisi', which he started writing as prison notes, continued to inquire into this phenomenon and attempts to show how bad governments affect people's lives.

"Kihoro's 'Never Say Die', late Wahome's 'Three Days on the Cross', Prof. Ngugi's 'Detained', Prof. Mkangi's 'Walenisi' and other books within this genre should be taken seriously as studies in paranoid regimes."

"Throughout the 1980s, Western countries were promoting the respect of human rights in the world, which were most abused in one party systems in Eastern Europe

and Africa. Single party systems had communism as their theoretical model. The fall of the Berlin wall in 1989 signified the collapse of this model, and the logical consequence of this was collapse of single party systems in Africa..."

Dr. Kamau Kuria, Constitutional Lawyer &

CHAPTER FIVE

James Opiyo: Master of the Dark Arts

Those who had an encounter with James Opiyo, the man who headed the team that carried out the Nyayo House 'interrogations', describe him as a well-built, reasonably good-looking person who could pass for a top-executive in the corporate world.

But looks, as they say, can be deceptive, and this is exactly the case in regard to not just Opiyo but also his deputy in the 'terror squad', Joseph Muinde. Both Opiyo and Muinde can be described, based on their appearances, as soft spoken and mild mannered.

The two were the kind of people who would only call you by your first name and even try to reason with you, taking time to explain why you should cooperate with the interrogators.

"Hata sisi hatufurahii kuona mtu mzuri kama wewe akisumbuliwa hivi" ("We are also not happy seeing a nice person like you being harassed this way.") Colleagues who worked with Opiyo within the Special Branch or latter on to be renamed Directorate of Security Intelligence (DSIS) say he was a deeply religious person who regularly attended service at Nairobi's Seventh Day Adventists (SDA) church, near former CID Headquarters every Saturday. It was, and even today, popularly known as Maxwell SDA Church.

Opiyo was a huge man who had small lower front teeth extracted in accordance with an old Luo tradition. He is said to have attended Migori and Homa Bay secondary schools both in the large South Nyanza before joining the police force (and ultimately the Special Branch).

While in the police force, Opiyo got to know the late powerful Permanent Secretary in charge of Provincial

Administration and Internal Security, Hezekiah Oyugi, with whom he struck some rapport. The good chemistry between Oyugi, Opiyo and the last Chief Justice in the Moi –KANU era, Bernard Chunga (then Deputy Director of Public Prosecution) (DDPP) was extremely useful in ensuring the ruthless success of the crackdown and subsequent torture of "Nyayo House Police Station" dissidents.

After the Mwakenya suspects were tortured at the Nyayo House basement to a point where the "Torture Squad" were convinced they had nothing else to confess, they would be taken to the Nairobi Law Courts often at dusk, where they would find one of the four or so selected magistrates waiting to 'hear' their case. These were the then pliant magistrates who would allow Chunga and the Special Branch officers to accompany the 'accused' to their courts.

Pleas of torture by suspects would fall on deaf magisterial ears. Acting almost like Pontius Pilate in haste to wash their hands off the blood of innocent victims, the magistrates would quickly mete maximum sentences prescribed by law for the alleged crimes and dispatch the suspects (now "convicts") to maximum prisons such as Kamiti, Naivasha, Manyani and Shimo La Tewa.

At this point, Chunga, Opiyo and his torture squad would leave the court smiling for a job well done. The relationship between Opiyo and the late Oyugi, during those days is said to have been very cordial and close that at the height of the Mwakenya crackdown, Oyugi helped Opiyo buy a house in Nairobi's Golden Gate Estate and acquired a Peugeot 504 station wagon, besides assisting him (Opiyo) construct a moderate permanent house in his rural home.

Opiyo's family is said to have originated from Alego area of Siaya District and settled in the larger South Nyanza (Migori District) near the late Oyugi's Rongo home (Rongo District).

Before Opiyo took over as the boss of the dreaded Terror Squad, he had previously worked in the external Intelligence gathering department of the Special Branch. When the "Terror Squad" was at the end of the 1980s, Opiyo is said to have been posted to North Eastern Province, where he worked until his retirement from the Public Service a couple of years ago.

In retirement Opiyo is, however, said to have changed his identity for purposes of concealing his past. He is no longer the dreaded James Opiyo of the infamous Nyayo House Police Station; but your rather humble citizen by the name James Obunga, still living in the larger South Nyanza, engaged in sugar-cane farming.

Torture Chambers Visited, February 11, 2003

The 25-storey building in the heart of the Kenyan Capital, Nairobi is named Nyayo like the vanquished Moi regime. It houses several government offices notably Immigration Department and lately the Registration of Persons, the Nairobi Provincial Administration Headquarters where the area Provincial Commissioner's (PC) offices are located.

In the same building was housed the Special Branch Police Force before it was disbanded. It was officially known as Directorate of Security Intelligence (DSI). Its premises were on the 10th, 15th and 25th floors.

The 25th floor was where interrogations were conducted. Interrogation, if I can quote *Sunday Nation* columnist Gitau Warigi (Sunday View) February 16, 2003, "interrogation is a very prime word for the savage torture that went on there. The small rooms were sound–proofed; while the curtains were all black!"

Other offices of the DSIS include the basement floor; where the notorious torture cells were located which was where "torture victims" (survivors) were allowed to visit the cells by the National Rainbow Coalition (NARC) administration on February 11, 2003. The survivors (including the author) were escorted by the then Nairobi Provincial Commissioner Cyrus Maina.

Some of the survivors broke down in tears at one point as they recalled their suffering, torture and that of their friends at the hands of the disbanded Special Branch Police (now the National Security Intelligence Services - NSIS) in the 1980s and early 1990s.

The blackened walls of cells at the basement, the hose-pipes, and the whips tell their own story. There was a control box at the basement of the torture chambers (cells) which was used to regulate into the cells the flow of icy water, or to blow hot dusty air into the torture victims or cold water. The torturers had their pick (Gitau Warigi wrote correctly in his *Sunday View* column of February 16, 2003).

February 11, 2003 was a day which will not be forgotten by the torture victims (survivors) and their families and friends, apart from the Kenyan populace who were able to see and view the chambers and revelations of what Nyayo House building was like through both the electronic and print media.

Why? The Nyayo House phenomenon is different. It was the first time Kenyans were seeing evidence of a government building which was deliberately designed for torture and degradation of its citizens.

The contractor who put up the building was quoted in the media as having told journalists that he was informed by the government officials that the basement structures were some kind of strong rooms, knowing how governments like being secretive plus the fact that they do have plenty of legitimate stuff they like keeping in secure storage, the contractor left it at that. Did the torture victims deserve the cruelties they suffered? The unequivocal answer is No. Not even the vilest crime justifies this kind of torture, not even murder. The law brings its own punishments up to and including hanging. The worst aspect of it is that the Nyayo House victims were being brutalized over some amorphous thing which nobody has proved actually existed.

By the time we were being taken to court we were completely broken men, our eyes (see one of my court pictures) were bulging in fright like caged animals. The magistrates and prosecutors who handled our cases would assume a fake air of disinterest, towards these wrecks brought before them and inquired softly and kindly if we were guilty.

Of course, by just looking at the victim, quite often with sores all over the body especially the legs as a result of staying in water and beatings inflicted by the torturers.

The legs more so the feet, were at that time out rightly in a state of rotting from the prolonged stay in water-logged cells, the men of the law knew precisely what the answer would be.

Hardly ever we were allowed to engage defense counsel(s). At the Law Courts (in the court room) surrounding and looking around you (read: the torture victims) are the cruel stares of the torturers who invariably would be full in the courtroom. We would turn to the magistrate and whisper or talk in low tones, almost inaudibly but with terrified urgency. *"I am guilty"*.

Many, including this author, pleaded 'guilty'. The reason was in fact simple. Better spend years at Kamiti Maximum Security Prison than a day more at Nyayo House basement torture chambers. Many of the torture victims whom I know were pretty harmless souls. Their lives and their dignity were crushed forever right there through the bludgeon of the state.

I know one Wallace Gichere (now late) who was once a first rate photo-journalist with *The Weekly Review* news magazine. For him, he was flung out of his fourth floor apartment window in Nairobi's Buru Buru Estate by the dreaded torturers. He has since been paralyzed and because of his health status he has had no secure source of income. I know those who got maimed permanently, while some died at the torture chambers and have never been compensated.

There are many like photo-journalist Gichere who passed-on poor and left their ravaged families in despair. There are those like the author, who have never got regular employment and who have been in the state of torment and harassment since they came out of incarceration.

Many prominent Kenyans went through the torture chambers. They include Kenya's second Prime Minister Eng. Raila Odinga, the late Assistant Minister for Internal Security Lawyer Mirugi Kariuki, former Nakuru Town MP) Lawyer Kamau Kuria, Lawyer Wanyiri Kihoro former Nyeri Town MP, Dr. Willy Mutunga renowned Law professor (now Chief Justice), Njeru Kathangu (former Runyenjes MP) the late George Anyona (former Kitutu Masaba MP), , Abuya Abuya former Kitutu East MP and Electoral Commissioner of Kenya, Prof Edward Oyugi, the late journalist/playwright Wahome Mutahi, Wahome's brother journalist Njuguna Mutahi, a former East African Standard, Nakuru Bureau Chief, now Managing Editor with *The People* newspapers. Mugo Theuri.

Below are names of some of those who went through the Torture Chambers:

1) George Moseti Anyona (former MP, political firebrand- now deceased)

2) Prof. Edward Oyugi (University don)

3) Augustine Njeru Kathangu (former Air Force Officer, later MP, now in politics)

4) Musa Cheparer (Political Activist)

5) Koigi Wa Wamwere (Political Activist, former Assistant Minister, now author)

6) Rumba Kinuthia (Lawyer, Political Activist- detained)

7) Ngotho Wa Kariuki (University don – detained)

8) Mwaura Kinuthia (Political Activist)

9) Harun Thungu Wakaba (Political Activist)

10) Geoffrey Kuria Kariuki (Political Activist)

11) Gibson Kamau Kuria (Lawyer, Political Activist)

12) Wanyiri Kihoro (Lawyer, Political Activist, detained – later MP)

13) Gitobu Imanyara (Lawyer, Political Activist, Editor, detained – MP)

14) John Khaminwa (lawyer, political activist, detained)

15) Mohamed Ibrahim (political activist/lawyer)

16) Gathitu Wa Kariuki (political activist)

17) Prof. Maina Wa Kinyatti (University don, later detained and fled to USA)

18) Mukaru Nganga (University don, later detained, now deceased)

19) Titus Tito Adungosi (Nairobi University student leader jailed – died in prison)

20) Kariuki Wangondu (political activist, lawyer cum journalist)

21) Israel Agina (political activist – detained)

22) Kimani Wanyoike (former MP, political activist)

23) John Maina Kamangara (political activist – deceased)

24) Gacheche Wa Miano (Law student – jailed)

25) Robert Wafula Buke (student at Nairobi University, jailed, now political activist)

26) Raila Amolo Odinga (political activist, detained now MP & Prime Minister)

27) Charles Rubia (MP, political crusader, detained)

28) Kenneth Matiba (former MP, Minister, political crusader detained)

29) Wachira Waheire (political activist)

30) Andrew Kibathi Mungai (political activist)

31) Mwanga ole Seyeiko (political activist)

32) Gibson Maina Kimani (political activist)

33) Milton Chege (political activist)

34) Harrison Okongo Arara (political activist)

35) Wahome Mutahi (Journalist, playwright, actor, author, now deceased)

36) Kangethe Mungai (political activist - jailed 15 years)

37) Philip Tirop Kitur (political activist jailed 15 years - Human Rights Activist)

38) Harissson Githaiga Gicheru (political activist)

39) Sheik Aziz Said Limo (political activist)

40) Loli Wamba Kamau (political activist)

41) Stephen Mulili (political activist)

42) Charles Kuria Wamwere (political activist)

43) Wilson Awour Agonga (political activist)

44) Dickson Nabwire Namadoa (political activist)

45) Ali Amin Mazrui (political activist)

46) Kamonji Wachira (University don – detained)

47) Karimi Nduthu (political activist – jailed now deceased)

48) Efffermont Nganga (political activist)

49) Gupta Nganga Thiongo (student lawyer - jailed, a lawyer, now deceased)

50) Hassan Hussein Juma (political activist)

51) Rev. Lawford Imunde (political activist - jailed)

52) Paul Amina (journalist –detained back in journalism)

53) James Odthiambo (political activist)

54) Njoroge Waruiru (political activist - jailed)

55) Joseph Karauri Miano (political activist – jailed 4 years - deceased)

56) Kimunya Kamana (political activist – jailed 4 years - back in politics)

57) Mwangi Mathenge (political activist – jailed 4 years - back in politics)

58) Francis Nduthu Karanja (political activist jailed 5 years - back in politics and farming)

59) Samuel Kangethe (political activist)

60) Cyrus Gitari Muraguri (political activist)

61) Stephen Krop Moroto (political activist)

62) Micheal Lobuin Mena (political activist)

63) Samuel Toyoko Namedo (political activist)

64) Ayub Kirui (political activist)

65) Julius Mwandawiro Mghanga (student leader- Univeristy of Nairobi, political activist, jailed 5 years , later MP for Wundanyi)

66) Julius Miano (political activist - deceased)

67) Karanja Mbaraka (political activist/ businessman - deceased)

68) Karanja Ndune (political activist/businessman)

69) Peter Njenga Karanja (political activist)

70) David Wakairu Murathe (political activist, jailed 15 months later MP for Gatanga)

71) Patrick Ouma Onyango (student leader, later political activist)

72) C.A. Onyango (political activist)

73) Owour Ongiwe (political activist)

74) Peter Oginga Ogego (student leader, jailed for 10 years, later Kenya's Envoy – USA)

75) Dr. Adhu Owiti (political scientist jailed five years later MP and Minister for planning)

76) Mirugi Kariuki (lawyer/activist, detained later MP, Nakuru Town now deceased)

77) Hosea Gitau Mwara (political activist)

78) Maina Kiongo Godfrey (student leader, jailed for five years)

79) Joseph Kamonye Manje (lecturer KSTC, political activist, jailed five years)

80) Peter Young Kihara (political activist jailed four years, now deceased)

81) Dr. George Katama Mkangi (University don, detained now deceased)

82) Ochieng Kabasellah (political activist, musician - jailed - now deceased)

83) Philip Wanjau (political activist)

84) Gabriel Kariuki Mungura (political activist)

85) Hezekiah Ochuka (political activist, former air force officer)

86) Koigi Kariuki (political activist, jailed, brother to Wamwere)

87) Margaret Wangui Kinuthia (political activist)

88) Elias Mbugua Murugu (political activist)

89) Mrs. Mwaura Kinuthia (political activist)

90) Jeremiah Kamau Kiruri (political activist)

91) Joseph Odour Ongwen (High School teacher, political activist, development consultant)

92) Shem Oketch Ogola (Political activist, Banker, jailed)

93) Apiyo Onyange (political activist)

94) Owour Atieno (political activist jailed)

95) Dr. Odhiambo Olel (medical doctor, political activist, jailed for five years)

96) Odenda Lumumba (High School teacher, political activist, jailed, land consultant)

97) Silvanus Okech Owour Atieno (political activist)

98) Opanyi Mwai (political activist, jailed four years deceased)

99) Jimmy Omwega Achira (journalist, jailed for two years – media consultant, publisher/author)

100) Silas Awour Imbo (political activist)

101) Absalom Ombee (political activist)

102) Eliud Odumbe Ahao (political activist, now deceased)

103) Owinyo Agutu (political activist)

104) Nelson Akhahuka Muyela (political activist)

105) Oyange Mbaja (political activist, detained, deceased)

106) Odungi Randa (political activist)

107) James Odindo Opiata (student of law, political activist, three years jail now lawyer)

108) Stanley Waweru Kariuki (political activist)

109) Prof. Peter Anyang' Nyongo (political scientist - detained, MP and Minister)

110) Onyango Oloo (Nairobi University student, jailed, fled to Canada)

111) Njuguna Mutonya David (journalist jailed five years, back to journalism)

111) Danson Kabiaru Mahugu (political activist, businessman, jailed)

112) Karige Kihoro (political activist jailed 18 months brother to Wanyiri Kihoro)

113) Kimondo Kiruhi (MP and political activist now deceased)

114) Mugo Theuri Wanderi (journalist, jailed four years again back to journalism)

115) Herman Marine Nderi (former policeman, political activists jailed five years, back to politics)

116) Kaggia Mathenge (political activist jailed four years)

117) Fred Osoro Nyakundi (former Kenyatta University student leader arrested - jailed for 15 months)

118) Peter Momanyi (former Kenyatta University student leader arrested - jailed for 15 months, fled to U.S.A)

119) Onchiri Nyakundi (former Kenyatta University student leader arrested - jailed for 15 months, fled to U.S.A)

120) Wafula Wekesa (former Kenyatta University student leader arrested - jailed for 15 months)

121) Kariithi (political activist jailed three years)

122) Wanjohi Njoroge (political activist)

123) Benson Thiro Karanja (political activist - businessman)

124) George Kihara Michuki (political activist - businessman)

125) Tom Ojicho (political activist)

126) John Kiriamithi (businessman cum writer)

127) Macharia Kobo (political activist)

128) Dr. Muga Kolale (University lecturer)

Peter Oginga Ogego in court after conviction
and sentenced to 10 years

Pascal Wandera, hotelier arrested and spent
7 days at Nyayo House torture chambers

Dr. Wanyiri Kihoro a former Nyeri town MP

Wachira Waheira

Late Dr. Mukaru Ng'anga

Mwandawiro Mghanga a former student leader, UON
after conviction and sentence.

Kimunya Kamana a former Nakuru town mayor -
jailed for 4 years

George Anyona a former MP of Kitutu Masaba and
political fire brand

Salim Ndamwe, one of the founder members
of the original FORD

Prof. Maina wa Kinyatti former Kenyatta
University Don now in the USA

Slyvanous Odour, arrested on September
25, 1986 and jailed for six years

Shem Ogolla Oketch, held at Nyayo
House Torture chambers for 45 days

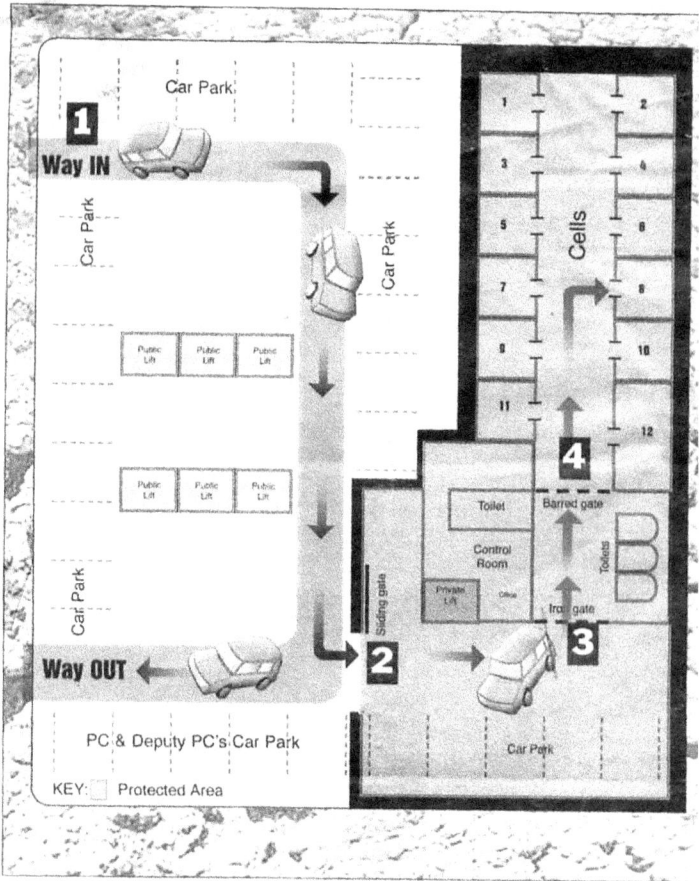

1 A vehicle carrying a blindfolded prisoner, makes its way into the basement	**3** The blindfolded prisoner is removed from the car and dragged past an iron gate into the holding cell area
2 A sliding electric door is opened by remote control. the vehicle reverses into a protected area.	**4** Door opens and the detainee is led and locked into a cell

Nairobi's Nyayo House housed torture cells and chambers. How the torture chambers/cells at Nyayo House appeared

CHAPTER SIX

Torture Chambers Exposed

The notorious torture chambers in the basement of Nairobi's towering Nyayo House were composed of twelve tiny cells.

The cells can be compared to the dungeons at the Gestapo torture chambers in Nazi Germany, while the interrogators were no different from sadists.

The Nyayo House Police Station cells were dimly lit and each had a tiny hole through which cool air was pumped through for the victims (occupants).

The walls, the floors and the door were painted – some black, some deep red. Each cell had an air tight metal door with a tiny lens through which a guard would monitor and see the suspects from outside, while from inside the suspect cannot see the guard.

There was no sharing of the cells like at the ordinary remand prisons or police station cells. The cells (chambers) had no natural ventilation and air was often pumped in at intervals – irregular. When you were in the cell you could hear the ration machines blow in.

Occasionally one could hear suspects knock and call out, "*We are dying... we are suffocating.*" This meant that pumping in fresh air had not been done! I was a victim a few times while I was locked at the chambers of the Nyayo House Police Station.

In those dark cells one only got a feel of sunshine or natural air when at the interrogation chambers, either on the 24th or 25th floor of the same building.

In fact, some of the victims or "Mwakenya suspects" spent long hours in the dark cells before they could be moved to the interrogation rooms, while others spent weeks before being taken to the courts to 'plead guilty' to trumped-up charges.

In the basement of Nyayo House there are two rows of the cells – six on each side. There were two open toilets – one with a door (used by guards), while one toilet was wide open and was used by suspects for long calls only. The 'suspects' passed water or urinated in their cells.

The cells were categorized into two – 'dry' and 'wet'. The wet ones actually were water-logged and were meant for the suspects who had undergone intense interrogation and had not 'cooperated'. Once the 'suspect' failed to yield to the whims of the interrogators he was to be consigned to the 'wet' cell and denied food and drinking water for two or so days.

All this depended on one's capacity to withstand hunger or starvation.

Normally the 'wet cells' were flooded with freezing water so that the occupants would not sleep.

The cell size was between three feet by six feet and six feet by six feet, although there were others which may have measured four feet by nine feet. One cell would not accommodate two mattresses of let's say three feet by six feet.

While in those cells and being a regular 'visitor' to the interrogator's torture chambers normally on the 24th and 25th floors of Nyayo House, medical care was unheard of. One was not allowed to bathe until the day you were set to be produced in court. The common features in those interrogation chambers were: rubber whips, wooden clubs, broken pieces of wood, burning cigarettes, cold iron tubes, rods and pins which were at times used to inflict pain on the 'suspects'.

In addition, pistols of all kinds were at hand and exposed or placed on the interrogators' tables. The essence was to threaten and instil unlimited fear on the 'suspects' which did not matter whether one had anything to say or not. Occasionally the interrogators would show or pretend to be friendly and offer the 'suspects' sodas, roasted pieces of meat or a cigarette for smokers. This was a rare gesture.

Many "Mwakenya suspects" left Nyayo House torture chambers and cells without exactly knowing where they were, this was revealed by many suspects when in prison, some insisted they were locked up at Nyati House – Headquarters (then) of the dreaded defunct Special Branch police unit.

This was so because the arresting officers would take one to any police station depending on where one was picked up or arrested. Then in many cases, the 'suspects' would be blindfolded and bundled into the back of normally white Land Rovers, which were not marked but attached to Special Branch police.

Then the journey that was meant to cause confusion started. But at the end of it all, the last or final destination was at Nyayo House torture cells or dungeons.

Actually, the Nyayo House torture chambers were those ordinarily for interrogation. Dungeons or cells were those on the basement – about two if not three floors underground, which served as police cells or prison remands, but there was no sharing like in prison remands or other police stations.

In most cases, all the "Mwakenya suspects" were blindfolded and driven into Nyayo House dungeons/cells in the night from wherever they had been arrested. The dungeons had two stages before one gets right inside: the second stage could be identified due to the screeching of the door when it was being opened.

The vehicle was slowly driven up to the second stage, after which the suspects were asked and assisted to disembark.

At the last and second stage, the 'suspect' was still blindfolded. The 'new guest' would be led by hand and accompanied by a Special Branch police officer and led into a lift which stopped in the basement. At the basement, a kind of gate was opened and you were received by two persons – assumed to be part of the Nyayo House interrogators. There was a desk, and one of the two took the suspects personal details or data, while one person kept watch around the information desk armed. This time you have been unblindfolded.

Upon finishing taking or recording personal details, for instance, if you have cash (money), wrist watch, spectacles, etc. are taken and kept for you.

At this point you were again blindfolded and pushed to the next entrance, which was dark but with dim lighting and one of the cells was opened and you were bundled inside. "*You would be there until 'wazees' (interrogators) come for you and you would tell them why you were brought here.*" The suspect was informed. In this case, you were consigned to the 'dry cell'.

The suspects were often blindfolded in their cells or dungeons before being taken out for interrogation sessions upstairs (24th or 25th floor). While at the dungeons no one communicated with another but all would hear colleagues groaning and screaming in pain from the neighbouring or adjacent cells, especially after an interrogation session upstairs, and while hose-piped water was being 'sprayed' on the suspects and at the same time the cell was being filled with water – which was normally very cold.

Ordinarily the ice-like water was to some extent a 'relief' for a suspect after torture during the process of interrogation.

Interrogation sessions were either carried out on the 24th or the 25th floor; and you would leave blindfolded and escorted from the basement cell and get bundled into the lift which took you in the company of your 'officer'. Most likely on arrival at the 24th floor, you were assisted or aided to walk up a flight of stairs, pass through an open space, where one felt the touch of sunshine and a whiff of natural air and noise of either hooting from motor vehicles on the road (Uhuru Highway) or the streets and avenues of the city many floors below. At this point, you were blindfolded.

Then one (suspect) was led into an interrogation chamber. In the first days of the interrogation sessions one was taken into the chamber which looked like a boardroom with a long round table. At one end, the seated person was most likely the chairman of the session.

The suspect, then still blindfolded or hooded would be made to sit on a chair at the centre of the room. Suddenly the hood was removed and the suspect would be face to face with a horde of well-dressed persons – Special Branch police officers.

The torture sessions would go on and on for not less than three days and later on you were handed over to two or three interrogators and towards the end (when you were about to be produced in court), you would end up with one interrogator .

Once you were with one interrogator, even the size of the interrogation room became smaller. The first lot of interrogators was normally between ten to fifteen led by none other than James Opiyo.

On the floor of the first mass interrogation, the common features were fresh blood spots – apparently meant to scare the suspects, that whatever went on there or had transpired before was that one was either injured or shot. Making the scene scarier, there were pistols on the interrogation table, while some of the interrogators hung pistols from their waists, deliberately for the suspects to see.

At the same time the floor was littered with planks from broken chairs to drive the message home. The interrogators sat in partial darkness, while the suspect was flooded with light. All sorts of weapons were displayed on the table to apparently scare and intimidate the suspect into admitting the allegations or accusations for that matter.

Some of the interrogators at this stage smoked continuously, others would eat either fried or roasted meat or chicken, while others pretended to be chatting as some cleaned their pistols! The whole scene and vicinity was so threatening and scaring.

The interrogators in the first instance sounded friendly, despite the scaring scene and intimidating environment. But, hell soon broke loose if the 'suspect' was deemed 'uncooperative' - being uncooperative meant denying or refuting claims and allegations that one was a member of Mwakenya or was involved in publishing or in distribution of the so-called 'seditious' publications known as Pambana, Mzalendo and Mpatanishi or refusing to name an 'accomplice' in the oathing or any of the involvement above (this author was a victim of the above claims).

Once declared 'uncooperative', you (the suspect) were ordered to move to the end of the interrogation room and strip yourself naked, prostrate yourself before the interrogators and exercise your body in a manner to expose your nakedness to the utmost humiliation and cause yourself dizziness.

At some stage, a suspect was asked to do push-ups, exposing your private parts (including the rectum) to the interrogators, some of whom just laughed as if they were in a pub or night club drinking. At times the exposed genitals would be in contact with the contaminated, dirty floor with blood spots.

The other 'gymnastics' was to rotate the body around the self from one spot, with the index finger touching the ground. This in essence and in the actual sense was meant to cause dizziness and eventually suspects lost balance and tumbled over – as the 'gang of interrogators' descended on you with all sorts of beatings ranging from kicks, whips and wooden clubs and planks from broken chairs, just what an angry swarm of bees would do to an intruder.

The gang of interrogators, who were often referred to as 'wazees' would beat a suspect until he 'cooperated' or else he would be taken back to the dungeons or cells at the basement with strict instructions to the guard(s) who were also police officers of lower ranks but from the dreaded, defunct Special Branch police unit.

At the dungeons, the instructions were to prolong the suspect's suffering. The exercise would go on so long as the suspect was conscious. Once the suspect lost consciousness, he was carried away and the next person, the suspect would see after regaining consciousness was an officer(s) who would pretend to be friendly and appear to be assisting him, by taking you away from the scene of torture while blindfolded to another torture chamber. This would even be after two days, at which the sessions would be carried out.

An 'uncooperative' suspect was in most cases taken away from the torture chambers, while blindfolded, straight to the dungeon/cell where the officers of lower ranks would hose him (suspect) with cold water under high pressure.

The officer would stand at a distance enjoying the experience as the suspect coiled up in a corner of the 'wet' cell, until water rose to the ankles or knees depending on the instructions given to him by the interrogators.

The suspect was then left submerged knee or ankle-high in water. The suspect would remain from 24 hours to 48 hours in that state. This actually depended on one's ability to withstand the kind of torture. At one stage, I recall having stayed in water ankle-high for two straight days without a meal, although I remember that I was served with a packet of fresh milk, while still in the 'wet cell'.

Tour of Torture Chambers

For the first time in Kenya's history, torture victims/ survivors toured Nyayo House – both torture cells and chambers at basement and on the 25th and 26th floors of the building.

Survivors were the first people to be allowed to tour

Nyayo House on February 11, 2003 before the torture chambers were opened to the public.

'A door slid open on February 11, 2003, which revealed a glimpse of independent Kenya's shameful past.' *Daily Nation* of February 12, 2003 reported.

A grey steel door, twelve feet wide that led to an underground car park that led to another steel door that led to a steel barred gate that led to the infamous torture cells of Nyayo House.

And their own blood was often the last thing the inmates saw as they were beaten senseless or dragged screaming to a bath of sulphuric acid that stood at the end of the corridor (see graphical drawing of the Nyayo House basement which contained the twelve cells and other related compartments)

The National Rainbow Coalition (NARC) government – through its Justice and Constitutional Affairs Minister Kiraitu Murungi, formally apologized to the survivors when he (the minister) joined a group of survivors who were allowed to return to the dungeons for the first time as free men.

The cells will be turned into a National Monument Of Shame and will then be opened to the general public, said the Minister.

The victims, escorted by the then Nairobi Provincial Commissioner, Cyrus Maina, broke down in tears at some point as they recalled their suffering and that of their friends in the hands of the disbanded Special Branch police (now the National Security Intelligence Services – NSIS) in the 1980s and early 1990s. They (survivors) broke promptly into songs and loud chanting as they relived an ordeal, almost too terrible to remember, on how they were tortured in the Nyayo House cells. The best estimates suggest around 2,000, of whom it is thought at least a quarter were killed, whereas the rest were thrown into jail or detention camps and for the most part forgotten, except by their loved ones.

But the records of this time are so unclear that the families of those who were killed still have no records of their deaths, they just disappeared. What terrible crime did they commit to deserve all this?

Their crime was not even to cry for freedom. In theory, it was that they had criticized the ruling party, KANU, -- by suggesting, or even to thinking that it might have been less than perfect in the way it (KANU) served the Kenyans.

It was called subversion – but it was as if the party slogan 'KANU builds the Nation' had become perverted to 'KANU destroys the nation'.

The methods the torturers used were simple, brutal and cruel. They would strip the suspects during initial interrogation, stab them in private parts and on toes, force them to stand on red-hot metal, stay in freezing drenched cells for days, suffer blasts of hot gristly air which clogged their nose and throat and even made one blind, drink your urine and even eat your faeces unknowingly.

The torturers would smash up furniture and attack you using the broken pieces of wood from furniture like wild beasts!

The victims faced all manner of accusations – ranging from possession of seditious publication(s) holding revolutionary ideas. The list is not exhaustive.

When a false confession had been beaten out of the survivor, one would be blindfolded and pushed in front of a court, often late in the afternoon – normally it was after 5:00 p.m., when no lawyers were available and one would face charges of subversion, sedition or treason for that matter. One would be sentenced at the dead end of the evening and be driven away to jail.

The journey to the cells began when one was picked up by the dreaded Special Branch police officers, blindfolded and thrown into the boot of a car or the back seat of the Special Branch Land Rovers – the short chassis Land Rovers were the most common vehicles used or assigned to Special Branch police officers.

First, one victim is booked in any of the Nairobi area police station cells and later picked from there after 8:00 p.m. in the entry to start the long journey through Nyayo House basement cells/dungeons. The Land Rovers often entered the huge grey gate in the wall of Nyayo House and into the underground car park beyond. One would remain blindfolded from the moment of arrest (if you were arrested at night) but if you were arrested in the day, blindfolding starts as the junior police officers attached to the torture squad would come for you from a police station to where you had been booked awaiting collection, normally after 8:00 p.m.

Arriving at the Nyayo House basement, the big doors slid open silently and revealed ferrying 'prisoners' (suspects) would reverse into the 'compound' where the alleged victim who was then blindfolded would be hurled out to start a long journey to prison through certain designated magistrates and prosecutor.

Interestingly, the section of the building that houses the heavily fortified deadly cells was designed along with the building and was never an after-thought!

Today, (after the time when they were opened to the public and torture victims – on February 11, 2003) some of the cells remain dark and empty, while others still contain literature that was ostensibly confiscated from 'prisoners', or that was used as supposed evidence during their interrogation. Most of that lay in heaps contained reports criticizing the vanquished KANU regime.

Other cells/dungeons contained ruined water pumps, broken wooden tables and chairs and disused steel filling cabinets.

Opposite the inner parking bay is a lift that shuttled exclusively between the basement cells and the interrogation rooms. The lift could take ten people at a time.

The VIP lift that serves the rest of the Nyayo House building also accesses the 26th floor which at the time

(February 11, 2003) torture victims who visited the building found that it contains only disused furniture. The windows and doors of the rooms are heavily grilled!

On arrival in the rooms, a suspect would be stripped naked and pushed into one of the twelve cells at the basement where he would be left in total darkness.

The terror one felt was intensified by what one could hear -- groans, entreaties for mercy, and screams of pain. For in those cells, someone would always be crying, screaming and begging for mercy and forgiveness!

The thick concrete walls are reinforced with steel rods and escape was impossible. It would have taken an armed invasion to achieve it. Next to the cells and at the side of the parking lot was a control room fitted with buttons that controlled wind and water pipes with outlets in each cell.

Through the outlets would be pumped very dusty wind that would choke and irritate the eyes and lungs. Sometimes freezing water was flushed through the hose pipes into the often sick, hungry and wounded torture victims.

The cells, designed to keep the 'prisoners' in complete darkness, were however, also fitted with a piercing bright light in one of the top corners that could be flicked on at will, another way to torture the terrified occupants?

The hose-pipe also used to flood the cells, leaving 'prisoners' lying in water for days on end, still lies in the compound. The journey to the cells/dungeons and torture chambers on February 11, 2003 by survivors began at the carpeted office of the then Nairobi PC Cyrus Maina. The PC denied that he had ever seen or been to the cells before, when he was approached by the survivors (including the author) and human rights activists late January 2003!

Genesis of Torture Chambers

A former lecturer at Kenya Science Teachers College (KSTC), Mr. Joseph Kamonye Manje was picked up from his office at KSTC, Nairobi on March 12, 1986 and driven to Kilimani Police Station, where he was then booked under the name 'Kamau'!

Days earlier, Special Branch police officers had searched his house and confiscated books, magazines and other related literature. Manje was later taken to Nyayo House where he says he was tortured for over two weeks and ended up at a Nairobi law court, and then proceeded to Kamiti Maximum Security Prison after he was convicted and sentenced to a five years' jail term.

Manje faced charges of being in possession of a seditious publication, 'Mpatanishi' (Reconciliator). He pleaded guilty before (then) Nairobi Chief Magistrate H.H. Buch, while the prosecutor was Bernard Chunga. Although Manje pleaded guilty he was remanded in custody until April 2, 1986.

Manje's jail term was reduced by the High Court ruling to three and half years, but conviction was squashed by the Court of Appeal after he had served three years of the sentence. The High Court ruled that Manje did not voluntarily plead guilty.

On that basis, Manje had enough grounds and sued the state over torture on February 14, 2003. Thanks to Manje for the action, this made the public aware of the genesis of the infamous torture cells or chambers at Nyayo House.

The infamous torture cells at the basement of Nyayo House, Nairobi were included in the original 1979 design for the government building.

The torture cells were shown on the architect's plan as twelve strong rooms to serve as the banking hall for the ground floor of the building and other government departments.

The action taken by Manje (then) to sue the government was the beginning of the revelation of exactly how the infamous torture cells and chambers came to be built.

The initial plan mooted in 1973, was to build Nairobi's provincial headquarters. A fourteen-storey model made in

1974 shows it would have been called Nairobi House and that basement was to be reserved for parking. And indeed, there are parking lots within the Nyayo House basement.

However, those plans were later on shelved and in 1977 a new blueprint for Nyayo House was designed by architects working for the then Ministry of Roads and Public Works and put up by a private contractor – Laxmabhai and Company at a cost of Kenya shillings 218,608,377.00.

Underground Chambers

The contractors were quoted by the mainstream media houses in February 2003, saying they were told that the underground chambers would serve as safes for storing or keeping 'secret documents' and 'cash' belonging to various government departments to be housed in the building once it was ready for occupation.

The specification for the walls and roofs of the strong rooms was a double wall –six inch thick each and sound proof material between them. The specification for the doors to the cells was five millimeter thick steel plates.

Laxmanbhai & Company Managing Director, Mr. Raghwani was further quoted by the press:

"We were constructing strong rooms. We were made to believe that various government departments would be using them. We only heard several years later that the rooms had been turned into police cells and torture chambers".

They had converted the rooms into torture chambers with freezing water or blasting prisoners with hot gristly air.

The media accessed the Nyayo House architectural plans with the approval of Cabinet Minister Raila Odinga, who was once held in the cells and whose then ministry -- Roads, Housing and Public Works. --maintained all public buildings.

The plans of the building show that the lift from the cells and the torture chambers was originally designed to access all 25 floors of Nyayo House building.

But a note was made on the building plan in 1980 indicating that all doors from the lift were slabs, except those to the basement and to the 5th, 10th, 15th and 25th floors. It is not clear who made the note but the Managing Director of the construction company said that they were told they were to ensure the lift served 'only those government departments which needed access to the strong rooms, those with cash and secret documents to keep'.

Interestingly the 5th floor was, and still is, the office of the Nairobi Provincial Commissioner and other senior officers of the Provincial Administration. The other three floors – 10th, 15th and 25th are said to have housed Special Branch police (non-uniformed police unit), which has since been re-named the National Security Intelligence Service (NSIS)

The Twenty-Fifth Floor

The 25th floor recalled by Nyayo House torture survivors as Interrogation Office was initially designed to house the building's caretaker with a dining room, a kitchen, a lobby, servant's quarters, two bedrooms and a store.

The house (25th floor) became the interrogation centre, where victims were often tortured to confess to crimes they knew nothing about. They were then thrown into the lift and returned, while blindfolded to the basement cells/dungeons where their ordeal began all over again.

On February 11, 2003 when a door opened to reveal a glimpse of independent Kenya's shameful past, the twelve cells or dungeons; each eight feet by ten feet and seven feet high are painted either black to absorb all light or a dark enveloping red, the colour of blood.

The underground chambers (cells) were declared a protected area, through a legal notice of February 1, 1979 remained a state secret until the veil was lifted on February 11, 2003 and survivors (including the author) and journalists were allowed in.

National Council of Churches of Kenya (NCCK) on Nyayo House Cells

The opening of the torture cells/dungeons to the public was on February 11, 2003, which was described as the first window let into a dark part of the country's history.

The Rev Mutava Musyimi, Secretary General of National Council of Churches said, *"It was fitting they should remain open as a museum to show the gross abuse of human rights Kenyans were subjected to in the past (during the Moi-KANU Era)."*

The then N.C.C.K. Chief Executive was quoted by the media as saying *"Many Kenyans had for years refused to believe there were such torture chambers in Nyayo House and warned that unless the country confronted the uncomfortable realities of its history, it could not heal."*

Interestingly, no action has since been taken to confront the uncomfortable realities of Kenya's history according to the Rev Musyimi who joined mainstream politics in the 2007 General Election and elected a Party of National Unity (PNU) MP for Gachoka Constituency.

What has Hon. Musyimi done in regard to Nyayo House torture chambers or was he speaking for purposes of scoring political mileage then? How come he is not advocating for needed justice now that he sits in the August House?

Raila Odinga: Approved access to
Nyayo House Architectural plans when
he was a Cabinet Minister. He was also
a victim of the torture chambers.

CHAPTER SEVEN

Mwakenya: Trials Were a Travesty of Justice

Through the decades of 1980s, machinations by politicians and security agents came up with claims of dissident movements that were out to topple the government then headed by Daniel Arap Moi of KANU.

The most demonized suspect was a shadowy group called Mwakenya. Soon after the August 1, 1982 coup attempt, the government ordered a country wide crackdown on Mwakenya and other associated dissidents.

A former powerful Permanent Secretary (P.S.) in Office of the President, Hezekiah Ogango Oyugi, gazetted a police station. Reason being: so that a Special Branch police unit (non-uniformed police force) mandated to interrogate suspects could hold them there. The police unit was equipped with white Land Rovers 110, which were distinct from the usual government blue police Land Rovers.

The vehicles would pick up suspect(s) from any part of the country without referring to the local police division and deliver them directly to Nyayo House Police Station. But, at times, if one was picked or arrested in the day, one would be booked at the nearest police station or if the suspect was from within Nairobi or the environs of Nairobi one was booked in any of the Nairobi area police stations until it got dark, then was to be picked and delivered to Nyayo House basement after being driven to so many places to cause some confusion.

The late Oyugi, who was the right-hand man of Moi, did not only equip the Nyayo House Police Station with white Land Rover 110s, but also posted officers then known as Special District Officers (SDOs) to every district in the country, who were detailed to report directly to Oyugi on the political climate from the ground. The SDOs were just 'spies' briefing Oyugi on any suspected dissidents and spying on their bosses – the District Commissioners (DCs) and Provincial Commissioners (PCs). They even spied on the government officers like the District Police Officers (OCPDs). They were normally very arrogant with a lot of money to spend and nice new cars (mainly Nissan Sunnys). The motor vehicles usually had private registration numbers and they were usually self-driven. At that time, this category of civil servants was feared by all government officers. In fact, it is on that basis that some government officers ended up being arrested, interrogated and sometimes taken to court or detained on fictitious charges.

This time around, the hunt for Mwakenya was on in earnest but the question that remained unanswered was whether the group was real or a phantom created as an excuse to crack down on alleged dissidents or personal political enemies.

Kenya became virtually a police state like Romania and East Germany. The ground of choice to hunt for alleged dissidents were the public universities and institutions of higher learning, the focus being University of Nairobi (UON) and Kenyatta University lecturers and student leaders.

As a result of the crackdown on dissents in the universities, institutions of higher learning and in the legal fraternity, the media houses started taking on the mantle of criticising the government.

In the University of Nairobi, the alleged dissident students secretly authored leaflets and distributed them at night and posted them on walls at strategic positions and locations.

These leaflets got their way to media houses (both print and electronic) newsrooms. I do recall well. It was not unusual for the reporters and editors in print newsrooms to receive such leaflets or pamphlets which were greatly criticizing the Moi-KANU government for dictatorial tendencies and bad governance.

The security apparatus, which was heavily represented among the students and lecturers, used the publications to arbitrarily arrest suspects and accuse them of belonging to Mwakenya. In fact, many a times, there were Special Branch police officers who were pretending or masquerading as students in various faculties. Some of them ended up "graduating" or "repeating" for several years.

The leaflets that became famous then were *Pambana*, *Mpatanishi* and *Cheche*. Student leaders (then) like Kitur Tirop, who later became the chairperson of Release Political Prisoners (R.P.P.) were mercilessly grabbed from the main campus (University of Nairobi) by big squads of police and taken to Nyayo House basement for interrogation. Later on it goes without saying, Tirop ended up behind bars after being convicted on tramped-up charges of causing destruction of Kenyan property.

The government acted with obvious paranoia every time a new publication was launched and banned it. Being caught with it in your possession was interpreted to mean dissent and instant arrest and incarceration at Nyayo House Police Station, but in actual fact, it was Nyayo House basement cells or dungeons.

Hundreds of innocent Kenyan's blamed falsely by the security forces of belonging to Mwakenya were arrested, often at night, and taken to Nyayo House basement cells. Many of those arrested ended up being convicted and sentenced and were consigned to Kamiti Maximum Security Prison, although later they were moved to other prisons in the country, mainly Naivasha, Kisumu (Kodiaga main prison) and Shimo-La-Tewa (main prison).

Police would often break down doors at night, proceed to search homes and offices of alleged suspects without a warrant and 'find' either copies of Pambana or Mzalendo that the suspect himself had never seen in his house or office.

The suspect would go missing for days, even a month as the family mounted a search in all police stations. Then one evening he would be produced at the Nairobi Law Courts after 5:00 p.m. and be charged before a magistrate.

The magistrate would be Chief Magistrate Joseph Mango (now deceased). Applications by lawyers would often go to a particular Judge - Justice Norbury Dugdale, while the prosecutor would often be (Deputy Director of Public Prosecution (DDPP) Bernard Chunga, who later became Chief Justice but was forced to resign when National Rainbow Coalition (NARC) government came to power on December 30, 2002. He resigned in February 2003. He did not want to wait for the President to appoint a tribunal to investigate his conduct as per the allegations made by various groups, among them Civil Society and the media, especially the mainstream media houses.

In fact, most of the suspects, having been subjected to inhuman treatment at Nyayo House, were eager to plead guilty and be sentenced to prison, which was more 'friendly' than Nyayo House Police Station. No one left the torture chambers unscarred in body or soul. Many died while undergoing interrogation at the torture chambers.

At this point, let me remind you who the Mwakenya magistrates were, and presiding Chief Justices.

The Magistrates were Chief Magistrate H.H. Buch (late), Chief Magistrate Omondi Tunya (who later became a judge of High court) and Fidhahussien Abdullah. The late Chief Justice Allan Hancox was the presiding Chief Justice during the period/trials of the alleged Mwakenya dissidents.

The magistrates were often and normally referred to as The Four Mwakenya Magistrates

CHAPTER EIGHT

Torture Squad of Shame

It is not possible to list or name all those who participated and facilitated the evil activities and programmes that were undertaken at the alleged Nyayo House Police Station, which the late powerful Permanent Secretary, Hezekiah Ogango Oyugi, gazetted shortly after the August 1, 1982 attempted coup.

However, the author was able to obtain the names of some of the perpetrators – Nyayo House Torture Squad of shame. They are:

1) James Opiyo (Head of the Squad)
2) John Mburu (PSBO, Nairobi then)
3) Joseph Muinde (Deputy Head to Opiyo)
4) James Kilonzo
5) Ismael "Sam" Chelimo
6) James Gachanja Kariuki
7) David Wachira
8) Christopher Karanja Kiarie
9) Ben Machiri Kinguru
10) Petkay Miriti (PSBO, Nakuru)
11) Washington Kimumum
12) Elias Mjomba
13) Francis Ndirangu (interrogator of the author)
14) Samuel Muthee
15) Muchiri Wanjau
16) Jacob Katama (Chief Inspector, cautioned and charged the author after 45 days of stay at Nyayo House torture chambers/cells/dungeons)
17) Gerald Ndungu (Supt. Ndungu- then District

Special Branch Officer, Kisii) and was the arresting officer of the author)

Petkay Miriti: He was elected MP and appointed assistant Minister for Trade and Industry (2002 – 2007)

18) Leonard Wachira (Supt. Wachira, author's interrogator)

19) Ben Machira (late)

20) Timothy Kamunde (late)

21) Kieti

22) Ngericha

23) Machini

24) Kigeni

Hezekiah Oyugi's Operation Think-Tank

Following the August 1, 1982 coup attempt, Oyugi, the country's (then) Internal Security Chief, started chairing evening meetings with some close aides at his Harambee House Office – Office of the President -- to plan and strategize on how to go about and containing "new threats to the state security."

The late Oyugi had his own operational network (think-tank), which included the following:

1) Joseph Kaguthi (Personal Assistant to Hezekiah Oyugi in-charge of Security matters.)

2) K. B Ogara Oketch (Personal Assistant in charge of Provincial Administration)

3) John Wilson Ndiah (Personal Assistant at large).At one time he was a District officer (DO), Manga Division (Kisii then) before he was moved to Nairobi, Office of the President (Oyugi's office).

4) Nyagah Wambora (Personal Assistant in charge of finance, Oyugi's office)

Oyugi: Powerful P/S who was In-charge of
the Internal Security docket

5) Benard Chunga (gravitated around Oyugi's political orbit and often consulted with Oyugi and the Oyugi Think-Tank at Office of The President.

6) James Opiyo (Assistant Commissioner of Police (ACP), who was in charge of the intelligence network of the late Oyugi country-wide.

He later on, during the infamous Mwakenya crackdown and trials, was in-charge of the then discredited Nyayo House police-based torture squad. Its formation and constitution was masterminded by the late Oyugi, who at the trying moment of his life on Earth was an abandoned friend of Moi-led government and Moi himself, who had previously treasured him during the trying moments of the KANU Government.

Kaguthi: Personal Assistant to Oyugi, in charge of Security Matters (then)

Magistrates/Judges Who Handled 'Mwakenya' Related Cases

It was as if the Moi-led government under the umbrella of the ruling party KANU, and the only registered political party in Kenya (then), assigned specific magistrates, judges and prosecutors to handle the so-labeled cases.

The following featured during the Mwakenya crackdown era in the 1980s:

1) Chief Magistrate H.H. Buch (late)
2) Chief Magistrate Joseph Mango (late)
3) Chief Magistrate Omondi Tunya (late). He later

on was judge of High Court of Kenya.

4) Chief Magistrate Fidahussen Abudullah (late).

He was later on appointed judge of High Court of Kenya.

5) Justice Hon. Bernard Chunga. He was later to become Chief Justice of Kenya. He was also briefly in the NARC administration, but in February, 2003, hardly two months of the NARC administration, he disgracefully resigned to avoid a tribunal which had been appointed by President Kibaki to look into his conduct, following a petition by then Justice and Constitutional Affairs Minister, Kiraitu Murungi.

6) Chief Justice Allan Hancox (late), before he became Chief Justice, some of the Mwakenya-related cases and those of sedition were brought before him.

Retired President Moi Owes Kenya an Explanation

For a long period, the government building known as Nyayo House enjoyed the singular notoriety of housing elaborate torture chambers in its basement in the 24th and 25th floors of the same building.

The torture chambers were not known to the public except for those who went through there (including the author). Stories about the dungeons and cells were not taken seriously; only until February 11, 2003, when the gates to the torture chambers were opened wide to the torture victims in the company of (then) Justice and Constitutional Affairs Minister, Mr. Kiraitu Murungi – thanks to National Rainbow Coalition (NARC) administration.

Nyayo House was not just a place where the Provincial Administration Headquarters and a host of government ministries were housed. Once again thanks to a former legislator for Nyeri Town, Hon. (Dr.) Wanyiri Kihoro, for his book "Never Say Die" and a few others like playwright/ journalist Wahome Mutahi's "Three Days on the Cross"

In the book "Never Say Die," an account of what went on in those torture chambers would appear to be unbelievable. But that came to be known as the truth.

For those in government, claims and allegations of torture at Nyayo House Police Station, were always rebuffed as scabrous speculation and dismissed with withering comments.

This disconnection between real knowledge and government truth made the horror of Nyayo House socially distant – until February 11, 2003, when the doors to that dark past were flung wide open.

The pictures and television footage of the holding cells brought what Kenyans had all along suspected into the open. Clearly, the very large section of the building's basement reserved for torture and torment was not an engineer's after-thought.

The dungeons at Nyayo House were not akin to the extension a greedy landlord makes to the servant's quarters (SQ) to create a money-spinning guest house.

Air ducts, capacity to hold water to an adult's waist, cells made to measure, bathrooms, toilet, heat control centre, steel doors, black paint on the walls - all these things or gadgets were methodically planned and thought out not in colonial Kenya, but in 1980 (during Moi-KANU regime).

Nyayo House torture cells/chambers, also known as dungeons, were custom-built for breaking the bodies and the spirits of those who dared to think differently from the government, and to stray from the 'Nyayo' (footprints) of the then president, Daniel Arap Moi.

It is a building whose foundation had been well thought out and its uses methodically planned. Tax money was spent building this hideous 'Monument of National Shame', according to Kiraitu Murungi - the first Minister of Justice and Constitutional Affairs in the NARC Administration.

Nyayo House was built as replacement to the then dreaded and forbidding Nyati House on Loita Street, Nairobi that housed the Intelligence Headquarters and it was not a state secret.

The Nyayo House Police Station torture chambers are where suspected peddlers of sedition were taken to the courts (some on stretchers) as late as after 6:00pm to plead guilty to crimes they had not committed.

It is unbelievable that a man of Benard Chunga's Intelligence (I believe he was intelligent and it is on that basis he became Kenya's Chief Justice until February 21, 2003), when he was suspended by President Mwai Kibaki to pave way for the tribunal that was set to be established, in order to probe him.

The question here is, did he not see anything wrong or unusual in the way the Nyayo House victims were brought to court and in the way they pleaded guilty without a fight, while all of them (victims of Nyayo House) were not represented? If he did notice those anomalies and decided to look the other way, his sense of objectivity, according to Kwamchetsi Makokha, clearly exceeds the requirements for the job of the country's Chief Justice. Makokha, who was then writing for the *Nation* newspaper said: "*It would verge on indifference*".

With the truth before the public after steel doors of the torture chambers were opened wide on February 11, 2003, it was not hard to understand why former political prisoners and detainees were so charged about Chunga being the Chief Justice, when NARC took over the state instruments of power.

It actually took the then NARC government less than two weeks (ten days) to have Chunga suspended as the Chief Justice to pave way for his probe. Writer Makokha had several questions which he raised in his write-up in the *Daily Nation* of February 14, 2003. Among the questions were:

"*Should Kenyans believe that in all the time that these things happened, the Latter-Day Saints in NARC government did not know about them? Many leaders in the new NARC government were in positions of power and knowledge; would it be nearer to the truth that they were not aware?"*

Writer Makokha further wrote and appealed to all those good men who kept quiet when evil flourished to come forward and speak. They should tell Kenyans about their cowardice and about their ignorance. He added:

"It is not normal to torture people. And it is not normal for people to beat the daylights out of suspects in the course of police investigations. The things that went on at Nyayo House were not normal. They will never be normal at any stage. They are sickening and degrading. They were crimes against our very humanity."

On the other hand, writer Makokha argued in favour of the torturers by writing,

"Perhaps the policemen (read: torturers) picked to run the then Special unit for their sadistic nature might plead that they were only doing their job. Perhaps the then Deputy Director of Public Prosecution (DDPP), Benard Chunga, too, might say he was merely doing his job to prosecute people who were pleading guilty so eagerly if only to avoid being returned to the torture chambers/ dungeons. Perhaps Daniel Arap Moi would like to say that he too was just doing his job by making sure that there wasn't a murmur of dissent when he ran Kenya as a head of state."

Those mitigations, according to writer Makokha, are however, insufficient even before they are pleaded. The head of the Torture Squad – James Opiyo -- needs to talk about how proud he was of the service he gave to his country in those years he bashed in skulls, broke limbs, water-hosed detainees, served them and terrorized them out of their wits before the torture victims were consigned to Kamiti Maximum Security Prison through certain specified courts and magistrates in Nairobi.

With this truth before the Kenyan public, the people who were in charge of the Internal Security in those years and are still alive owe Kenyans an explanation. For this Nyayo House shame is not going to be swept quietly under the carpet so that it becomes a monument, a national relic. If anyone thinks that opening of the Nyayo House torture chambers and letting the victims cry their hearts out will serve a great national catharsis, they will have grossly miscalculated the nation's capacity for forgiveness.

Writer Makokha warned, *"Burying this history is the intellectual equivalent of trying to swallow an elephant. People need to take personal responsibility over what happened on their watch."*

Moi, as much as he is retired and enjoying his retirement benefits and other riches accumulated during his 24 years of rule, owes Kenyans an elaborate explanation as to why his government thought it was necessary to create this hell where people were abused, maimed, killed, executed, and tortured. He cannot pretend ignorance because these complaints came up in open court and in memoranda from International Human Rights Organizations for a long time. Each time, Moi would just ignore them.

Quotes from politicians and political scientists, citing world trends, say the retired president Moi owes the nation an explanation why the torture chambers existed and whether he (Moi) knew that the so called 'dissidents' were being tortured.

"In all the places where dictatorial regimes have collapsed, from Romania to former Yugoslavia to Argentina and Chile, living dictators are being asked to account for the errors of their regimes. So should we in Kenya," a University of Nairobi Political Scientist, Prof. Peter Wanyande, said in the *Sunday Nation* of February 16, 2003.

"Some police officers went too far and should be held to account." Saying he was ashamed when he saw the torture chambers following the opening of the Nyayo House Police

Station.

The public in fact needs to know if the government ordered intelligence officers to torture prisoners. Moi owes the nation an explanation, if he knew about the torture. *"If the government did not order the torture, they (torturers) must be held personally responsible. We need a forum where these things can be discussed."* Boniface Mghanga, Voi former MP and an ex-civil servant known for having composed songs in praise of Moi-KANU era, raised the issue in parliament during a debate on whether to compensate Mwakenya victims.

"They cannot say they were just doing their job. The President and the Cabinet must have been aware that the torture was going on. There must have been a cabinet resolution that there would be a crackdown", David Murathe, a former MP for Gatanga (1997–2002) was quoted saying. He added: *"Overzealous officers went overboard and hunted down and tortured people to justify their perks or pay."* Murathe was himself a victim of Nyayo House torture chambers.

"I think they had a blank cheque to pursue dissidents. They wanted the process prolonged so they could continue earning money and promotion(s). The torturers were sick sadists. They had tasted blood and kept wanting more."

Leaders, survivors and scholars argue that neither the torturers, nor the government officials, including retired President Moi, can seek protection behind the excuse that they were carrying out their duties by torturing fellow Kenyans, saying that they were dissidents.

"Former Special Branch Boss James Kanyotu (now deceased) and the Head of Torture Squad James Opiyo should come clean and tell Kenyans and the world over to what extent Moi was involved in these affairs." Runyenjes former legislator (1997–2002), Njeru Kathangu stated: *"It is not sensible to say Moi did not know. In 1986, he (Moi) talked in public of those who were arrested while they were talking*

like parrots. Moi knew what was going on." Kathangu added, while contributing to the debate in parliament.

The culprits should be given a chance to confess and cleanse themselves through a Truth and Reconciliation Commission, which the government had pledged to set up. Solutions lie in the future. Revenge, recrimination and retribution will not help the country.

A Truth Commission will give the victims the opportunity to forgive their tormentors; families of those who died in the process of torture can forgive the culprits. *"Victims would be seen to have been done justice"*, Raila Odinga, a cabinet minister then stated, when he visited former cells in torture chambers on February 14, 2003. He spent ten days in the torture chambers in 1988 and two days in July 1990 en route to his third detention stint. He is now the country's Prime Minister in the coalition government of Party of National Unity (PNU) and that of Orange Democratic Movement (ODM).

CHAPTER NINE

Mwakenya, a Creation of the Moi Government

Soon after the August 1, 1982 coup, plotters had been locked in, and the exercise of weeding other plotters out of the armed forces, led by the late powerful Permanent Secretary in Office of the President, Hezekiah Oyugi started in earnest. Oyugi, soon after, had become the most talked about and powerful civil servant in charge of the country's Internal Security docket and a master player in power games then.

"Around the same time, the country had become something of a political pressure cooker without any safety valve to let out the pressure," Sunday Standard political analyst Mwenda Njoka wrote. He added: *"Opposition to the government was treated like treason. As a result, any dissenter or opponent of the government was to be picked if not arrested and interrogated for purposes of obtaining information to assist the government in being in power."*

It is in fact, under these circumstances, that Mwakenya, a movement that was reportedly bent on overthrowing the government, is said to have been born.

"There are those who maintain that Mwakenya never existed in reality but was a creation of the country's political establishment and security apparatus meant to suppress any legitimate dissent to the government and mask its failings." Njoka, who was then writing for the *Sunday Standard* on political issues argued.

Nevertheless, sources within the security network, Njoka said, still remained firm that indeed Mwakenya only existed (and allegedly later as an aftermath) of the August 1, 1982 coup attempt.

Whatever the truth on the issue of existence and the alleged state security threat then posed by Mwakenya, one thing here is clear: such a threat (irrespective of whether true or imagined) was just to ensure that the powers that were maintained their place in the sun.

When it came to power games, the late Oyugi was as smart as they came. Being Internal Security Chief, he was one of the few individuals with unlimited access to President Moi (now in retirement after 2002).

Having closely followed the investigation methods used to crack down on the coup plotters closely-knit network, Oyugi knew perfectly well how the same methods could be used in maintaining political control even after the immediate danger of the coup attempt was over.

It is perhaps from this understanding of the dynamics of Kenyan politics that the country's then Internal Security Chief started having evening meetings with some close aides at his Harambee House Office to plan and strategize on how to contain "new threats to the state security".

The late Oyugi had his own operational network. At that time Oyugi's aides were Joseph Kaguthi (then Personal Assistant in-charge of security matters). He later became a Provincial Commissioner (PC), K. B Ogara Oketch (the Personal Assistant in-charge of Provincial Administration), John Wilson Ndiah (then Personal Assistant at-charge). Another key personality who gravitated around Oyugi's political orbit at the time was Benard Chunga (who later on became Kenya's Chief Justice during Moi-KANU Era).

Within the country's intelligence network, Oyugi's operational man was the dreaded torture master James Opiyo. During the Mwakenya crackdown period, Opiyo was a regular "visitor" to Oyugi's third floor office at Harambee House (Office of The President). It was through Oyugi's patronage that the team that Opiyo headed managed to have access to so much money, enjoy unlimited operational latitude and was able to strike terror in the heart of almost anyone who heard they were on his case.

The Nyayo House Terror Squad was so dreaded that at the height of its power, then a Cabinet Minister or an MP would be scared to death if anyone told them that 'Opiyo's boys' were enquiring about him. It reminds me of an incident when 'Opiyo boys' went for the then MP for Kitutu East (now Kitutu Masaba) Abuya Abuya, who later became a commissioner with the defunct (disbanded) Electoral Commission of Kenya (ECK) and picked him up from around Parliament buildings.

Abuya, who served the defunct ECK until October 2007, was picked up by 'Opiyo boys' and put in the white Land Rover, then driven to the Nyayo House Police Station but passed through other places, for him to be confused as to where he ended up and held for interrogation.

When at the torture chambers for a weekend, one would hear Hon. Abuya Abuya (this author was also in the chambers when Abuya was brought in) scream.

After about two days, Hon. Abuya was driven out of the dungeons and dropped around parliament buildings. He may never erase the experience he underwent that weekend after being picked up from Parliament buildings by the 'Opiyo boys'.

It was not surprising that given the kind of terror, it had brought about in the country; the Nyayo House Torture Squad at some stage diversified its operations to include extortion and settling personal scores. The former MP for Subukia and a former Assistant Minister for Information and Communication, Koigi wa Wamwere, who himself is a graduate of Nyayo House torture chambers and cells tells of a story in which his brother-in-law went through the same dungeons before being released. The condition(s) was to give Kenya Shillings 15,000.00 to James Opiyo. Koigi told the torture victims meeting (also attended by the author) in Nairobi on February 18, 2003 that when the brother-in-law delayed to deliver the 'cargo' to Opiyo, somebody was sent by Opiyo to collect the Kshs 15,000.00 and indeed Koigi's brother-in-law had no option but to part with the money.

Late Oyugi, too, was not left behind in occasionally using the Opiyo team to 'teach' those who had crossed his path a lesson or two in humility when dealing with the 'Big Pen' as he had been nicknamed. He was a topmost civil servant and powers within him were so immense that his pen was enough to send you packing – sack you or terminate your services without much ado.

Torture Methods That Shamed Spanish Inquisitors

Like gory tales of the 15th century Spanish inquisition tribunal that was established or set up by the Pope to mercilessly combat former Jews and Muslims and those accused of crimes such as witchcraft or sorcery, an encounter with the Nyayo House Torture Squad was an unforgettable lesson in human endurance to pain.

The first Spanish Inquisitors were so brutal in their methods of extracting information from religious traitors that Pope Sixtus IV had to intervene. But alas, the Spanish King had found a weapon 'too precious to give up' and the efforts of the Pope to give the inquisitions a human face thus failed.

Spain's first grand inquisitor was known as Dominican Tomas de Torquemada, who was so ruthless that he is today the symbol of the dark era of inquisitions.

Torquemada would torture his victims with physical and psychological pain in small but very effective doses. His cruel and methodical torture techniques are classical examples of prosecution from which many latter days Torquemadas have learnt their trade.

The ultimate inquisition tool intended for maximum terror in others was called 'burning at the stake' where the victim was tied to a cross and burnt alive.

Of course, Kenya's Torture Squad never reached the heights of Torquemada. Nevertheless, some of the

Nyayo House torture chambers/cells would have taught Torquemada some lessons too.

Anatomy of Torture

Use of torture as an interrogation weapon, they say, is as old as interrogation itself. Torture is one of those things many countries do but rarely ever want to concede that it is part of its interrogation tools.

It is like something almost everyone does when it suits them. Everyone knows that everyone else is doing it or capable, but adopts a not-in-my-backyard attitude when the 'T' (torture) word crops up. Even in open democratic states like the USA, torture of suspects has been used when it serves 'national interests'. In 2002, the USA government was accused of employing torture methods to pry information out of suspected Al Qaeda terrorists being held (then) in Guantanamo Bay in Cuba.

In Kenya, it is an open secret that torture has been extensively used by many other arms of the country's security apparatus. But, perhaps no one beats the Criminal Investigations Department (CID) arm of the Kenyan police when it comes to devising ingenious torture methods that leave no tell-tale signs.

In terms of volumes, on any given day even during the night, officers were likely to torture many more people per day than those that went through Special Branch police and its Nyayo House dungeons. But, since more often than not, most 'customers' of the CID are hard-core criminals; the extreme torture methods employed by this police department often go unnoticed by the general public.

This, in fact, means that the defunct Special Branch Police Unit was likely to attract much more attention for each individual it touched than a dozen or so who underwent similar torture in the hands of CID, quoting sources well versed in security matters *Sunday Standard* of February 23, 2003 reported.

Official Position of the Government

The Moi government crackdown on perceived members of the underground Mwakenya movement which reached its peak in early 1986, had different faces, but the government had its official stand. There was a countrywide hunt for the people, mostly university lecturers and radical student leaders and professionals such as lawyers and journalists.

"And if the movement was for real, perhaps the distribution of the organization's, publications -- Mpatanishi' and Mpambana gave the Moi-led regime the justification to crackdown, prosecute and put behind bars those perceived as radicals, opposed to the Moi regime." The *Sunday Nation*, March 12, 2000 commented in its write-up titled "The Mwakenya Files".

Suspects were rounded up after being accused of various clandestine activities ranging from being members of Mwakenya to publishing and possessing the illegal Mpatanishi and Pambana, the *Sunday Nation* reported.

The publications' distribution, which had also reached its peak in 1982, drew angry reactions from the Moi-led government, the ruling party KANU (the only legal political party at the time). Party leaders, professionals, and trade unionists then strove to outdo each other in the condemnation of Mwakenya and the alleged authors of the two publications. It did not matter whether they had seen or read the pamphlets. Effigies of the alleged authors were burnt in some parts of the country.

The crackdown intensification by the Moi-led government saw a cross-section of Kenyans -- including primary and secondary school teachers -- end up as causalities. Factory workers, university dons, student leaders, civil servants, messengers, professionals in the private sector were arrested, hurriedly prosecuted and bundled to jail but without being subjected to torture in the basement of Nyayo House Police Station.

In most cases the suspects were taken to court during odd hours, charged and jailed all in a day and without an opportunity to seek legal representation. Jail terms ranged from 15 months to 15 years, although the majority got jail terms ranging between three years and five years; a few exceptional cases received jail terms of ten years and 15 years.

Some suspects would be charged with 'seditious intents', attending or participating in meetings the purposes of which were to raise funds for an intended 'congress' which was then to be called Mwakenya National Congress, and being in possession of a draft programme of 'Mpatanishi', a publication of a movement and circulation aimed at inciting, causing discontent and discrediting the popularly elected, government led by President Daniel Arap Moi.

The Nairobi Chief magistrate, H.H. Buch, who heard almost all the Mwakenya and other related cases, would sentence suspects but not before telling them that they were not handicapped by ignorance or any other factor in agreeing to be both members of the 'illegal' group and being in possession of the publication(s).

KANU, which was the only legal political party and the target of clandestine movements, was supposedly scared to the bone by the emergence of Mwakenya and the distribution of the organization's publications – Pambana and Mpatanishi.

At the height of the distribution of the alleged publications in early 1986, a KANU Governing Council meeting under the chairmanship of Daniel Arap Moi, came out strongly like a wounded tiger, condemning all those behind the "subversive" movement and the authors of its literature.

The 1986 April meeting instructed all the ruling party (KANU) branches countrywide to be vigilant in detecting the 'dissidents'.

The party's top policy-making organ accused the movement of aiming at retarding socio-economic development in the country and accorded the government 'fullest' support in dealing with the Mwakenya menace.

The then Minister of State and Internal Security, Office of the President, late Justus Ole Tipis had earlier told parliament that police had arrested the 'brains' behind Mwakenya.

The late Ole Tipis noted: *"The government would take stern, necessary and appropriate action against those bent on subverting the 'good government' of Kenya, legally constituted under the laws of Kenya."*

Mr. Tipis, who was in charge of Internal Security, had been asked in Parliament to clear the air regarding Mwakenya's existence in the country and that it was allegedly a threat to the peace of the country and its citizens.

It was not clear to most legislators and Kenyans whether the alleged organization existed in the real sense. Many were of the opinion or view that Mwakenya and the December Twelve Movement (DTM) were just a creation of the Moi-led government to justify the crackdown, prosecution, jailing and detaining of perceived government critics, who were often labelled as 'dissidents' or anti-Moi or anti-KANU.

Therefore, the official position of then Moi-led government was that Mwakenya as a movement and other related clandestine organizations, whose activities and programmes were meant to overthrow or bring down the legitimate KANU government, were to be cracked and dismantled as per the KANU Governing Council Meeting.

Moi: Chaired the April 1986 KANU Governing
Council Meeting at which "Mwakenya"
activities were condemned.

CHAPTER TEN

Genesis of the Special Branch

The history of Special Branch police dates back to the pre-independence days when the colonial government created a department or unit within the police force for gathering intelligence on matters related to politics.

It is this beginning that gave the department the unsavoury reputation as the police unit exclusively for oppression and suppression of the free will of the people.

Over the years, the department operated under the wing of the police force with the police commissioner as the overall head. This has since changed with the transformation of the Special Branch from a police department into a professional intelligence gathering outfit.

The spy chief, James Kanyotu (now deceased, while in retirement) was the first African head of the Special Branch. He holds the record of the longest serving Director of Special Branch, having worked from independence and under two presidents – the late Mzee Jomo Kenyatta and the retired president Daniel Arap Moi.

The late Kanyotu retired early 1993 and was replaced by William Kivuvani, who after a rather short stint was succeeded by Brigadier (Rtd) Wilson Boinett. Kanyotu and Kivuvani came from Central and Eastern provinces respectively, while Brig. (Rtd) Boinett was from Rift Valley.

Over the years, the Special Branch operated under various names although during most of the period, its operational methods remained basically unchanged until a few years ago. From 1970, the Special Branch was technically changed to Directorate of Security Intelligence (DSI) through a presidential charter.

The late Kanyotu, First Director of Special Branch
After Kenya attained independence

However, even with the changes, the name "Special Branch" remained in most people's minds. The presidential charter was renewed in 1979 and the DSI operated under it until the enactment of the National Security Intelligence Service Act in 1998 (NSIS).

The NSIS was established as an independent civilian agency whose mandate was purely advisory to the government. As a civilian agency, it meant that the intelligence unit was no longer under the command of the Police Commissioner but headed by its own Director General, who reports directly to the president, but liaises with other government officials on a need-to-know basis.

The new Act also stripped NSIS of powers of arrest and interrogation, leaving it to concentrate on gathering and analyzing intelligence on any threat or potential threat to the national interests of Kenya.

An interesting aspect of the NSIS Act is that it never provided any transitional clause for continuity or transfer of officers, functions and powers from Directorate of Security Intelligence (DSI) to NSIS. In fact, this left NSIS to make a clean break with the past and shed off any excess baggage it would have inherited from the Special Branch and DSI and start literally on a new clean political slate.

The creation of the NSIS meant the actual disbandment of the DSI and creation of a completely different outfit which recruited officers from private and public sectors.

When DSI was disbanded, all the officers who had worked with the directorate had to quit their jobs to enable the new outfit to make fresh recruitment.

Some of the officers were later re-employed while those who did not qualify to join the new intelligence service were returned to the police force where they were either retained or retired.

The NSIS used the interlude between the demobilization of DSI and its formation as an opportunity to off-load most of the intelligence officers whose track record(s) did not fit the 'new look' of the outfit.

That Kanyotu's Special Branch had a hand in seditious pamphlets speaks loud. The unit ceased to collect or analyze information, and turned into an arresting agency.

One day in 1987, intelligence officers picked up a prominent figure in motor rallying circles from his Limuru home, north of Nairobi for interrogation at the dreaded Nyayo House Police Station then referred to us Nyayo House offices of the Special Branch. And Mr. Stephen Mbaraka Karanja was never to be seen again - dead or alive. When he went missing for too long, his family applied for a writ of habeas corpus.

High Court Judge Derek Schofiled ordered the police to produce him in court, but was told that police could not comply because Mr. Karanja had died in police custody – that he was shot while he allegedly tried to escape.

The judge demanded that police, (Mr. Kanyotu's Special Branch was then a division of the Kenya Police), produce his body.

What followed was a grisly exercise as police exhumed 19 bodies at the Eldoret Municipal Council cemetery in search of the victim's body.

An angry Mr. Justice Schofield described the episode as callous and demanded an explanation from the Commissioner of Police and the Director of the CID.

Instead, he was swiftly removed from the case and transferred to an up-country station by Chief Justice Cecil Miller. But the judge rejected the transfer and opted to quit, later leaving the country to take up office as the Chief Justice of Gibraltar.

It was not until much later that it emerged that Mr. Karanja had been shot and his body burnt to ashes at a forest near Eldoret Town. A witness to the incident was to recall his last words to have been: *"There is no God in Kenya!"*

Mr. Karanja was just one of many Kenyans in the mid-1980s who were victims of the dreaded Special Branch, which was the lead security agency operating in total disregard of law in pursuit of perceived dissidents.

Mr. Karanja had been arrested in connection with a clandestine dissident movement called Mwakenya.

Kenyans first heard about the group in 1986. It was said to be the offshoot of another clandestine group called the December Twelve Movement. The latter sprang from the blues in 1983, immediately after the abortive military coup the previous year. Both were alleged to publish seditious leaflets called Mwakenya/Mpatanishi and Pambana, respectively.

A retired senior intelligence officer now reveals that both Mwakenya and its seditious pamphlets were creations of Mr. Kanyotu's intelligence system, while the December

Twelve Movement and Pambana were creations of a parallel intelligence system run by Internal Security Permanent Secretary Hezekiah Oyugi.

The two men were bitter rivals competing to impress President Moi on who was more effective in keeping dissents at bay.

The retired intelligence officer traces the birth of the December Twelve Movement and Mwakenya to the early 1979 when the Government grew increasingly worried about growing radicalization of staff and students at the University of Nairobi.

In 1982, President Moi re-introduced detention without trial and locked up three lecturers, Mukaru Ng'anga, Edward Oyugi and Kamonji Wachira.

But dissent in institutions of higher learning went on unabated, and intelligence came up with Pambana, says the retired officer.

This is how it worked. On identifying the 'troublesome' lecturer or student, intelligence would plant some Pambana leaflets on him.

He would then be arrested and 'made' to confess to belonging to the shadowy organization called the December Twelve Movement, the purported authors of the offensive literature.

Dozens of students and lecturers were arrested and jailed after being forced to confess to membership in the dissident movements.

Many at the university, in fact, were keen to get their hands on the seditious publications and distribute them to like-minded friends unaware that they were only spreading the net of those to be arrested.

The operation went hay-wire, says the officer, when Mr. Oyugi formed a parallel intelligence system, which deployed 'Special District Officers' across the country to report directly to him.

The net had then spread from academia to include lawyers, journalists, politicians and businessmen. The targets would be held incommunicado for two to four weeks and tortured at Nyayo House.

On being brought to court they were ready to confess to anything. The court appearances were invariably early in the morning or late in the evening, outside normal working hours.

The unrepresented suspects would always be dragged before a succession of Nairobi Chief Magistrates who would soon after be made judges.

The prosecution would be conducted by Deputy Public Prosecutor Benard Chunga, later to become Chief Justice, while always hovering in the background would be the dreaded Intelligence Officer James Opiyo of Nyayo House torture chambers.

How the Terror Squad Was Formed

Emerging fresh details about the notorious Torture Squad that worked at Nyayo House horror dungeons in the 1980s reveal that the terror unit was given an unrestricted green light to crackdown the suspected dissidents immediately after the 1982 coup attempt, *Sunday Standard* political analyst. Mwenda Njoka reported in the edition of February 23, 2003.

According to Mwenda Njoka's in-depth analysis, it was established that although the intelligence unit squad had been in dormant existence since independence, the 1982 (August 1) putsch was used as an excuse to give it a carte blanche on political dissidents.

The government may only have initially intended to get to the bottom of the coup and to arrest all suspects involved, both civilian and armed forces, but the unit's given mandate survived long after to deal with real and imagined political dissident outside and within the Moi-KANU led government.

Although use of physical and psychological torture had been in existence, real brutal torture gained systematic political acceptance in the volatile days following the August 1, 1982 coup attempt, the *Sunday Standard* reported.

"It was after the coup attempt that some senior security officers within the Moi-KANU regime came up with the idea of using 'extreme measures' to get to the bottom of the revolt and also do whatever it took to prevent a re-occurrence of similar rebellion in the future." The *Sunday Standard* political analyst further argued.

That insurgency by the Kenya Air Force (KAF), Njoka says had the effect of waking Kenyan politicians and the country's security apparatus from their slumber and false assumption that 'it can never happen here'.

The mandate knee-jerk reaction was to try and control a complex political problem using simple methods where brute force was the weapon of choice: that is precisely when the torturers' services were needed.

As a result of the paranoia created in top political circles by the coup attempt; unprecedented crackdown of suspected dissidents started in Kenya on a scale only then known in the former communist bloc nations. Initially the unit that was later to be referred to as the 'Torture Squad' had in its ranks officers from the Special Branch (read: the National Security Intelligence Service), the Criminal Investigation Department (CID), regular police and the Armed Forces.

According to Njoka's findings, some of the meetings that led to the formation of the 'Torture Squad' took place in the Lanet area of Nakuru (home to some sections of the Armed Forces). This, in fact gives credence to reports of a close relationship between the unit and Armed Forces during its early days of its formation. The group was, right from the onset, given the leeway to use whatever method(s) it deemed fit to solve the coup attempt puzzle and in the process, maintain national security.

The investigators into the insurrection – who comprised of security officers from Special Branch, CID; Military Intelligence Corps (MIC) and the Military Police (MP) – got down to work. In the process, they started systematically torturing those they suspected of having a hand in the attempted coup or the attempt to overthrow the government. Soon, a whole new industry of inflicting unbearable pain to extract information was born – which later came to be known as 'Torture Squad'.

Even after the specific mandate of the interrogators was over, a new tool for maintaining political control had been developed and politically legitimized. It was out of these inauspicious beginnings that the unit that was later to be headed by one shadowy character by the names James Opiyo was founded.

This, in fact is the unit that owned the torture chambers, cells and dungeons of 'Nyayo House Police Station', where hundreds of Kenyans' (many of them innocent) suspected to have political opinions different from those of the then ruling elites were subjected to harrowing and sometimes fatal experiences during extraction of 'truth' through extreme bodily pain. Just how did the group gain its political legitimacy and who, besides James Opiyo were the other players?

When the Nyayo House Unit was formed, many seasoned Special Branch officers wanted to be part of the action. Here was an elite group of select officers given the task that appeared at the time not only politically glamorous but lucrative and perfect stepping stone to further one's career, if not to enrich oneself.

The political atmosphere at the time was such that curtailing anyone who appeared like a threat to the government was the perfect route to career progression in the police force, not to mention financial gains. This applied both to Special Branch officers and the politicians alike (a case of the late Kariuki Chotara). In Kenyan politics, Njoka continues to argue, it was then the era of witch-hunting reminiscent of McCarthyism and the hunt for communists in the United States of the 1950s.

During the formation of the unit, according to Njoka, not everyone within the Special Branch could be accommodated. Among the seemingly lucky ones then was James Opiyo, who was in charge of the 'Terror Squad' and his deputy Joseph Muinde.

These were the officers who sat at the apex of the 'Interrogation Unit' and made decisions that could mean either life or death for those unlucky enough to have attracted the unit's attention.

Another significant player in this scheme of things was the then Nairobi Provincial Security Intelligence Officer (PSIO), John Mburu. The PSIO was however, not directly involved in the day-to-day running of the interrogation unit. That task was left in the hands of Opiyo and his deputy Muinde.

Below Opiyo and Muinde were a cadre of other Special Branch officers dealing with various aspects of the unit's operations and activities or programmes. Among these were the real technical interrogators. These were the people who came into contact with suspects, in encounters that the lucky victims who survived would remember in dread for the rest of their lives.

Given the kind of work they were doing, it is not surprising that efforts were made to keep their identities secret as much as possible. Even today, few of those who went through their hands in the torture chambers, dungeons and cells of the so claimed Nyayo House Police Station have a clear mental image of those who tortured them.

Chatting with some intelligence officers who served in the Special Branch at the time, it came out clearly that when the unit was being given political backing and formal status, no one knew that the seemingly elite entity would later turn out to be another name for infamy not only for the Special Branch but more so for those officers who served in the unit.

The unit that was mandated to deal with political dissidence in the 1980s went by various names. To some, the team was simply known as 'The Interrogators' and to others 'Torture Squad'.

To be chosen as a member of the 'Task Force' was then viewed as recognition of one's professional ability within the Special Branch. After all, here was a 'major and complex political crisis' that needed solving and the assumption was that only the best were being called to serve.

"Those of us who were left out from this team really felt bad. For many of us, being left out appeared like your bosses were telling you that you were not good enough" recalls a former Special Branch officer. *"At the time, we did not know what exactly these people were doing. We only knew they were the most highly regarded by the government and they got everything -- money, cars, access to the people who matter in the government, you name it; they had it."* A former Special Branch officer was quoted in the media.

CHAPTER ELEVEN

Secrets of Moi–KANU Era Falling Apart

The most tightly held secrets of the Nyayo Era, started falling apart and have become known to people in Kenya, the Kenyan Diaspora and the entire world.

As steel door after steel door is forced open by men and women who suffered in what used to be torture chambers, cells and dungeons, the images and tales that emerge are those long associated only with the Gulag in the former Soviet Union, the torture chambers of Romania and the ones in Augusto Pinochet's Chile.

But every time the torturers were told that what they were doing had no place in Kenya, they got more vicious, just like they did when the prisoners asked whether the torturers were human according to accounts of the survivors (this author inclusive).

On February 11, 2003, February 14, 2003 and February 19, 2003, survivors of the horror of the Nyayo regime broke down in tears after they visited the torture chambers/dungeons and cells at Nyayo House basement.

The first lot visited the basement cells, the second lot, led by Cabinet Ministers also visited the basement cells and the 'secret offices and torture chambers' on the 24th and 25th floors of Nyayo House, while the third group visited both places on February 19, 2003, after they (survivors) had held a consultative meeting and formed a task force committee of eleven people.

It is no secret, victims died in the torture chambers, but the numbers will never be known. What is coming to be known is that the reasons for the arrests and subsequent tortures were flimsy and the conditions in the cells unbelievably brutal just like the torturers.

The victims were supposed to be revolutionaries out to overthrow the Moi-KANU led government. The evidence, like what they (torturers) found with some of the victims – 'American War in the Vietnam', 'A revolution in Zanzibar', Karl Marx write-ups etc. cannot constitute a threat to national security. The victims would end up at Nyayo House Police Station torture chambers for days, weeks if not months and were forced to do countless push-ups, lie on their back and lift and maintain their legs at 45 degrees to the floor. Those who could not sustain the exercises were whipped with pieces of wood from broken chairs on any part of the body.

Many torture victims would be charged with 'carrying a seditious publication', being a member of an underground movement -- for example Mwakenya, December Twelve Movement, had administered oaths, etc.

It did not matter whether the publication was Mwakenya or any other; all the time and charges stated were flimsy; being in possession of such publications, could earn one several days, weeks in the torture chambers, dungeons and cells and finally either detention or prison.

What Some Torture Victims Recall

i) **Joe Njoroge:** Was charged with possession of a seditious publication. He recalls that he stayed in the torture chambers for five weeks. Electric shocks and doses of cold water were splashed on him from a powerful hose pipe. He was offered no food for some days and thrived on drinking water on the floor which was mixed with his urine.

Njoroge was arrested on September 21, 1989 in Namanga, Kajiado District.

"The torturers said then that I was in possession of a magazine with a report titled 'Mwakenya Demands', I was bundled into the boot of a car and first taken to Central Police Station.

"I was then blindfolded and brought to Nyayo House. I was normally taken for interrogation at the top floor of the building. It was normally a panel of about 15 men who questioned me. For six straight days, I did not eat and I had to drink water that was flooding the cell! One evening I was quickly taken to court, charged with being in possession of a seditious publication and being a member of an unlawful organization. I was then convicted and sentenced to one and half years in prison and released in February 1990."

ii) **Wahome Mutahi:** In the same Nyayo House torture chambers, playwright/journalist Mutahi (now deceased) recalled being splashed with cold water from a powerful hose-pipe, and down with hunger, drank water mixed with his urine. Mutahi and younger brother Njuguna Mutahi, who was then an Information Officer (a Kenya News Agency Reporter) were arrested on August 9, 1986 and confined to the torture chambers cum-cells for 30 days.

The Mutahi brothers were later charged with failing to report a felony and were convicted and jailed for 15 months. Wahome recalled that he was held in the fourth cell to the left along the row of six. The walls were painted black, there were six cells in two rows thus each row had six cells. The basement had a total of twelve cells.

"It is a miracle I would return a free man and recall the dark days I languished here for no crimes committed." A former *Sunday Nation* columnist recalled.

"We were locked in the cells and splashed with ice-cold water from a powerful hose-pipe. Your body would be frozen, you would shiver and urinate in the cell; if you were lucky, you would be freed to go to the toilet within the basement under a police officer. The cells were always pitch dark and we only knew it was daytime when workers in the upper floor dragged their chairs and the way the torturers were dressed."

173

iii) **Silvanus Christopher Odour:** Was arrested on September 25, 1986 from his office at the Kenya Society for the Deaf Children (KSDC), Nairobi, then located at the Kenya National Theatre, Nairobi

"Two plain-clothes police officers wanted to talk to me. The moment I stepped outside, a third plain-clothes police officer appeared and they asked me to board a waiting Land Rover, which as usual, was unmarked. In the Land Rover, I was blindfolded and ordered to lie on the floor of the vehicle and stay still. I was taken to my house, where they carried out an intensive search through the books and journals. They took with them my passport, academic certificates and books like 'American War in Vietnam' and 'A Revolution in Zanzibar', I was taken to the cells and forced to do countless push-ups.

"I was beaten up and screamed and one huge officer stepped on my face. They beat me until I was bleeding from everywhere. I was returned to the water-logged cell and I was being splashed with cold water through a powerful hose-pipe.

"After 76 days of stay at the torture chambers, I was told that I would either die in the cells or confess and be taken to the court. I was taken to the court in Nairobi after 6:00 p.m. and the prosecutor was Benard Chunga. I was handed down six years, which I served at Kamiti Maximum Security Prison."

iv) **Gitobu Imanyara:** Lawyer/publisher of Nairobi Law, Monthly Journal had this to say:

"The cells were dark and noisy since there would always be someone screaming in one cell or another. The interrogators used the ventilators to blow in dust until we would be completely chocked. A few hours later, they would flood the cells/dungeons with cold water and leave you standing in it for several hours.

"I particularly remember a huge fat woman interrogator among the torturers. During interrogations they would offer you a cold soda but you couldn't take it when you had not eaten food for days!

"At one time, I was taken to Kenyatta National Hospital (KNH) for medical attention and I believe that there were similar cells there. All four of my limbs would remain chained while I underwent treatment and I would have no visitors.

"Many people died in those cells due to torture. The government should form a commission of inquiry to ascertain the exact number of people who died and seek ways of healing the survivors."

v) **Shem Oketch Ogolla:** He was picked up in August 1986 and held at Nyayo House for 45 days. He wept uncontrollably as he narrated how he was stripped naked, whipped and tortured.

"I was locked up in the third cell. I was stripped naked and thrown into a dark cell, after interrogation torture was regularly conducted and my cell was ever flooded with cold water.

"They ordered me to talk about myself from the time I was born until I was arrested. I was denied food, most days I was at the torture cells and chambers and at times fed on leftovers. I was at some stage ordered to strip naked while on the 25th floor waiting for interrogation. I would sit on a chair in front of over ten mean-looking officers. I was accused

of plotting to overthrow the government. I was accused of being a member of Mwakenya. I remember 12 officers simultaneously descending on me with sticks of broken chairs and metal bars when I denied the allegation. They put to me that I was a member of a clandestine organization –Mwakenya."

vi) **Wafula Buke:**

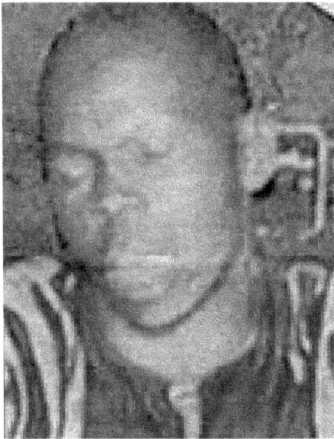

He was a University of Nairobi student. He was a student leader at the time of arrest. Buke was arrested on November 14, 1987 and detained in the torture chambers and cells for 16 days. He was later charged with being a spy for the Libyan Government and was jailed for five years.

He had this to say: *"I was jailed at Kamiti Maximum Security Prison before I was later moved to Naivasha and Bungoma prisons respectively. It was a tradition that when a prisoner completes his jail term he is moved to a nearest prison camp at his home district or province.*

"My appeal to the NARC government is to address the Socio-economic and political problems which prompted, the detainees to be on a war path with the Moi-KANU regime.

"Unless the problems are addressed and a solution found to the woes, the government might soon require house cells and torture chambers again like the Moi-KANU era did."

Buke asked Kenyans to remember all those who died or survived the enduring torture at Nyayo House Police Station. *"It appears these people tried to destroy history but failed."* Buke said in reference to the disused state of the cells and dungeons and torture chambers.

"All said and done, there are questions on whether the torturers should be made to answer and whether the former President Daniel Moi should be made to answer."

vii) **Mwandawiro Mghanga:** former MP (Ford People) for Wundanyi:

"The torturers would torture you and you would start to think that your life had lost all meaning, especially when they tell you that your children are equally being tortured by use of the recorded tapes.

"It is then as if there is nothing worth living for. When KANU lost, I felt like I wanted to cry. I don't see this as personal victory. It is justice for the thousands who went missing or got tortured at Nyayo House torture chambers, cells and dungeons.

"The torturers must be brought to book. They have to be found. It will take the country years to get over the Nyayo legacy. Finding out what happened to the victims is where we should begin."

Mwandawiro admits that he was a member of Mwakenya and participated in the production of Pambana a newsletter of the organization that was a thorn in the government's flesh.

viii) **Njeru Kathangu:** Former MP, Runyenjes

He had this to say:

"Mr. Moi knew what was going on and should be made to answer. Torturers should come out for we know them, to say exactly what their brief was. We would like to talk to James Kanyotu (now deceased), former Director of Special Branch and James Opiyo together with his accomplices (torturers) to tell us (the tortured) to what extent Moi was involved in this programme, whether Kenyans had the power or mandate to torture fellow Kenyans.

"I was first arrested on the eve of a visit to Kenya by former South African President Nelson Mandela, an act that made me think that Mr. Moi knew what was going on.

"The torturers should not escape an explanation on what the torture was all about and the torture chambers must be addressed fully.

"Orders can be given, and officers be asked to try to get as much information as possible from suspects; but that does not mean you remove the private parts of suspects. It does not mean you kill the suspects. Let these people come out and talk to Kenyans, otherwise they should be compelled to say it all out for Kenyans to know what took place at the so-called Nyayo House Police Station which housed the torture chambers, cells and dungeons."

ix) **Stanley Waweru Kariuki:**

It was November 14, 1988 at African Tours and Travel Trade Winds Hotel, South Coast when a contingent of policemen was ushered into the gates like any other guests. This was a tourist resort but the uniformed law enforcers were definitely not there for leisure. They were on a totally different mission; to crackdown on a Mwakenya suspect.

At exactly 6:30 a.m., Stanley Waweru was a wanted man. Kwale District DCIO accompanied by twelve Special Branch officers in five police cars whisked Waweru to the nearest police station. There he was held for hours. With no word from the officer who arrested him.

The following day at 6:00 a.m., he was blindfolded, thrown into a police Land Rover and taken to the Kenya Ports Authority Police Station. Waweru was worried because his three children, all below the age of six, were alone at home. His wife was attending a burial at her home district of Muranga and little did she know of her husband's predicament.

It was at that police station that he was told he was under arrest for being a member of the Mwakenya movement whose intentions were to overthrow the good government of President Moi. On the sixth day he was blindfolded and taken to an airstrip and was to be airlifted to Nairobi.

After almost one hour aboard a police helicopter, Waweru was untied, the blindfold removed and he was ordered to look out through the window. They were flying above the Indian Ocean and the mission was to drop him unless he revealed all that he knew of Mwakenya. Though terrified, he denied having any knowledge or links to Mwakenya. He was ruthlessly beaten unconscious. On regaining consciousness, he found himself in a cell at the Ports Authority Police Station where he stayed for another eight days.

Early in the morning of the eighth day, he was blindfolded, thrown into a police Peugeot 504 and driven to Nairobi, accompanied by six Special Branch officers. He was taken to Muthangari Police Station where he stayed for another eight days.

Again, police officers came for him at 6:00 a.m. They blindfolded him and loaded him into a Land Rover where he was laid down on the back. They took him round and round the busy Nairobi streets until he lost bearing of where they were or going. Finally he was taken to Nyayo House.

Waweru was left stark naked in a small room, water reaching his ankles and no communication from outside. Later, he was taken for interrogation by eight officers among them a lady officer. They occasionally descended on him with broken pieces of wood and anything at their disposal. He was humiliated by the lady who used to tickle his private parts. This lady would then burn him using a cigarette.

After 31 days of torture, he was ordered to accept all the accusations on the promise that he would get a non-custodial sentence. Having suffered physically and mentally, he decided to accept the accusation.

He was taken to court late in the evening. He stood before the magistrate and the prosecutor. Absentmindedly, he pleaded guilty to whatever charge read to him, his mind tasting the freedom which was so near. When the judgment came, it was five years in prison! He stood facing Chunga horrified and unbelieving, but the die had been cast.

x) **Wachira Waheire:**

"On December 2, 1986, Special Branch police officers came to my place of work in Industrial Area, Nairobi. They said they had orders to search my office. I allowed them but nothing was found. Later, they requested me to take them to my house and continue with their search. I used to live in Umoja estate. I accepted on condition that it would not take long.

"We boarded their Land Rover and went to my house. They searched for almost three hours. Inside my photo album, there was a press cutting entitled 'Desire for food is the cause of great political events'. They took it. They perused my photo album and took it also. They asked me whether I had a passport and I told them that I had. They demanded it and I gave it to them.

"The man who was leading them called me and whispered that I was under arrest. I asked him, very furiously why. 'You are a member of the outlawed Mwakenya movement. The evidence is with me.' He said. I was immediately blindfolded, thrown into the back of the Land Rover, ordered to lie down straight and taken to Jogoo Road Police Station. All the cells were emptied and I was thrown there alone. I was terrified. Later in the evening, I was blindfolded again, taken to a police car, and driven away.

"I remember the sound of a sliding door, total darkness and then I was all alone in a tiny room. They came for me again and we took a lift up. When they removed the blindfold, I was in front of twelve men. They demanded to know more about me. One ordered me to remove my clothes. I did, but hesitated to remove my underwear. He jumped on me, hit me on the head and I fell. I got up and removed it. The beating

started there. I have never been ruthlessly beaten like that in my life. One used a cigarette to burn me on my private parts and between my fingers.

"I was later put in the lift and taken back to my cell. Hot air was pumped in until I got choked. God knows what happened later. There was no food. I stayed for almost a week hungry. The beating went on even with no food. I was there for seventeen days.

"On the 17th day, I was taken up the lift again. A man whom used to be called Mzee read the charges for me. I later came to know that he was Mr. Opiyo. He said I was a Mwakenya member. I had failed to report the movement to the police. He also claimed that I took an oath at Umoja Estate binding me to the movement. I was warned that if I denied those charges in court, I would never leave Nyayo House alive. That was horrifying.

"At around 6:00 p.m. in the evening, I was carried before magistrate H.H. Buch. The prosecutor, Mr. Benard Chunga, read the same charges that were read to me at Nyayo House by Opiyo. Having in mind the warning I was given, I pleaded guilty. I was jailed for four years.

"For thirty two months, I was under segregation at either Kamiti or Kodiaga prisons. I don't know why I was being segregated. I used to be in the cell for twenty three hours. Half hour in the morning and evening were my only free time. I used to receive one visitor per month. The treatment at Nyayo House is unforgettable.

"The only thing that I can request the government is to form a Truth and Reconciliation Commission. Let the commissioners clear our names of the tag of criminality that was put on us by the former regime. I never knew of Mwakenya or Pambana. Those implicated in the torture, including the prosecutor should come out in the open before the law forces them to come out."

xi) Cyrus Muraguri:

"I stayed for five weeks in the Nyayo House basement. I was often interrogated by a group of about twelve men. They would beat me with pieces of wood; lock me in a water-logged cell with no food. The cell was extremely dark and never knew day or night. The squad that used to interrogate me was led by a Mr. John Mburu and his assistant was James Opiyo. Others were Christopher Karanja, David Wachira and Joseph Muinde.

"One of the things that I remember was the dry cell session and exercise. One would be told to do ten push-ups while being beaten at the same time. The officers were brutal and had no mercy.

"I was accused of being a member of Mwakenya movement and for having administered oaths on its members at my house in Muthurwa. They charged me with sedition in court, case No. 1399 of 1989. The magistrate was Mr. Joseph Mango, now deceased and the prosecutor was Mr. Benard Chunga. My case was not like the other ones conducted after official hours. It was in the day and I pleaded not guilty. I was remanded at Kamiti Maximum Prison until August 2, 1989 when Mr. Chunga entered a nolle prosequi because I refused to give evidence against my friends and I was discharged.

"My lawyers, Moses Wentangula, Zain N. Gathara, Wachira Kibanga and Mohammed Nyaoga were all set in court when the proceedings were to commence. I believe that the state knew of my innocence. The charges were only fabricated to de stabilize me politically, socially and economically."

xii) Pascal Wandera:

Special Branch officers casually dressed and others with dirty shirts went to the headquarters of Block Hotels in Nairobi. They introduced themselves to the manager who by then was one Pascal Omilo Wandera. They claimed that they wanted to see one of the staff at the hotel. Wandera resisted telling them to go and wait for their friend at his home. Being a busy office, Wandera could not allow visitors to the staff. They obliged and left.

After about 30 minutes, the same men now smartly dressed came back. They identified themselves, using IDs, as officers from the Special Branch. They were allowed to see the Director. They requested that the manager accompany them to their office for a few minutes. Being police officers, the boss agreed and Wandera was whisked away.

In the Land Rover, he was asked why he blocked them the first time. He explained, but one of them put it to him that he (Wandera) was blocking them from arresting a Mwakenya supporter. He was also accused of obstructing police officers while on duty. The Land Rover stopped near Nyayo House and Wandera was blindfolded. He remembers being carried in a lift to a floor near the top of Nyayo House.

He was taken before a group of interrogators who questioned him about his unruly and uncooperative behaviour. The men started to beat him using all kinds of weapons at their disposal. He was later the same day transferred to a small cell that was water-logged. That became his residence for the next six days without food or water to drink. On the seventh day, they came for him and asked him what he wanted. He said he wanted to go home. They put him in a Land Rover and drove him near his place of work. They ordered him out and one of the officers cautioned him never again to block them from arresting somebody or even getting somewhere.

A week at Nyayo House was the price he paid for obstructing Special Branch from arresting Mwakenya suspects. *"To me those were like seven years. What I went through was very inhuman"*. Wandera says with a look of great sadness on his face.

xiii) **Henry Ngila Kitwa:**

"At around 10:30 a.m. on July 7, 1987, I was on my usual duties at Kamiti prison. I was called from my block by the in-charge that morning. Usually, I was the head of E Block. I also used to deal with robbery and rape convicts and others who were classified as 'special category prisoners'. I had the privilege of meeting political prisoners during the Mwakenya crackdown.

"People like Raila Odinga, Gitobu Imanyara and Tito Adungosi were under me. I remember that Tito was a very good man – very social and talkative. On that particular morning, I was told that Special Branch officers had come to see me. I comfortably boarded their Land Rover and our next stop was at Muthaiga Police Station. Moments after arrival, they told me that they had arrested me. I was astonished. How could I be arrested from Kamiti without the knowledge of the head of prisons?

"I was thrown into a police cell. This was strange because it was my first time to be arrested. After some few hours the officer came and blindfolded me. I was shaking terribly. As they took me to a waiting police car, I knew that now I was on my way to die. I could not guess where we were heading to. They ordered me to lie flat at the back of the car that I guessed was a Land Rover.

Our next stop was somewhere with no light. The journey from Muthaiga to this place was long. As I was being pushed into the building, my blindfold was removed. Still, I did not know where I was, what time it was or why I was arrested.

"I stayed in this room for a considerably long period. The officers later came, bundled me into a lift to a certain floor. The room was full of chairs and curtains all over. Nevertheless, my eyes were sharp enough to peep between the curtains and see outside. I saw school children playing in a field. I grasped that this was a tall building and also that the school children must be from Catholic Parochial Primary School at Holy Family Basilica Church compound. My conclusion was

that I was at Nyayo House, a place I had heard people are tortured.

"In front of me was a group of men and one massive lady. At the extreme corner, there was a huge mzee who used to talk a lot of Kikuyu. During interrogation, this mzee was usually dozing. They questioned me about Mwakenya activities. I told them that I only knew of Mwakenya convicts at Kamiti. One man whom I later came to know as Mr. Opiyo shouted at me saying, 'You are one of them!'

"The other officers started beating me while others ordered me to strip. The lady concentrated on my private parts. She pulled my testicles as the men laughed. They pierced my nails using needles. This went on and on until I got to their interrogations and beatings. Every time I heard the sound of a lift at the basement, I knew that either they were coming to beat and interrogate me or another suspect was just from the same ordeal.

"The cells were no better. Hot dusty air was pumped in. I remember standing in water for a long time. Supply of food was minimal; in fact, I can hardly recall the number of times I ate.

"After 17 days, I was set free. This was on July 23, 1987 and I had not been charged and no reason for my arrest was given. They told me not to talk to anybody about what had happened else they would come for me.

"On August 10, 1987, I got my letter of dismissal from the prisons, which was dated July 24, 1987. I got no benefits. Verbally, I was dismissed on July 24th, and told to leave my home address so they would send my dismissal letter by post. Nairobi is like hell to me. I don't like coming here to see that building known as Nyayo House. I prefer being at my home in Makueni.

"One of the lessons I learnt during my training as a prison warder is that a prisoner is your brother. It's only that a misfortune has befallen him. Treat him kindly."

Kitwa treated sedition convicts kindly and for that, he was labelled one of them.

xiv) **Kimunya Kamana:**

At the age of 69 years, he was jailed for four years, when he was allegedly found guilty of administering oaths and failing to report to the authority. Although Kimunya, then the Nakuru District KANU Organizing Secretary, appealed against sentence and conviction, the appeal was not heard.

Kimunya, who was former Deputy Housing and Estates Officer with Nakuru Municipality until 1986, was arrested on January 2, 1987 and booked at Menengai Police Station, Nakuru for a day and driven to Nairobi blindfolded. On January 3, 1987, and ended up at Nyayo House torture chambers, where he was for 33 days. He recalls that he was among the invitees to State House Nakuru on December 31, 1986, when Moi warned against Mwakenya activities and ordered their arrest country wide.

Kimunya, who become Nakuru Town mayor after the first Multiparty General Elections of December 1992, when he was brought to court he sent shock waves throughout the country, especially within the ruling party – KANU -- when in his mitigation he told the court that during the alleged oathing ceremony, he had taken the oath together with the then controversial Nakuru District KANU Chairman, Kariuki Chotara and another KANU activist and State House operative, a Mr. Lasoi.

Kimunya further told the court that the KANU District Chairman warned, him not to disclose to anybody about the oathing ceremony, for it symbolized peace, love and unity.

This in fact caused the late Chotara to hide and it is alleged that he went for legal advice from a prominent constitutional lawyer, Dr. Kamau Kuria, although he was never arrested. But, it is claimed that he was interrogated by a team of police officers from the Nyayo House Squad.

In his response, the prosecutor, Benard Chunga, dismissed the allegations of Kimunya, as baseless and unfounded, saying that the accused was a jail bird and that the claims were a fabrication only meant to scare and psyche the court officers. In fact, Kimunya, from Agotui Location of Nyeri District was jailed for administering oaths, during the struggle for Kenya's independence.

He was sentenced to death alongside a former MP, Waruru Kanja. The two were released during state of emergency in December 1958.

Kimunya, who before he moved to Nakuru in 1959, served the life imprisonment term in 12 jail camps or prisons including Mageta Island prison camp on Lake Victoria, Kisumu. He was a member of Kikuyu Independence School Association (KISA), where he was a teacher between 1948 and 1950 and earned Kshs 25.

When he moved to Nakuru, he was enlisted with Nakuru Municipal Council in 1959 as Rent Collector and earned Kshs 165.35 - while still in the council Kimunya organized Nakuru District Freedom Fighters organization (NDEFFO) and spearheaded the organization's members to purchase land. NDEFFO purchased four farms within Nakuru District and distributed averagely ten acres each to its members.

Kimunya at one time was in the delegation from Nakuru to State House Nakuru and is on record to have told retired President Moi on the face that vote queuing system was not practical in Kenya as that was tantamount to taking Kenya back to the colonial era and Moi is said to have been very unhappy with him, although he (Kimunya) was the district's ruling party – KANU Organizing Secretary.

Kimunya, who was convicted and sentenced to four years on February 3, 1987, was accused of oath administration, failing to report of the existence of an underground movement – Mwakenya to the authority. And that for oathing charges, he is said to have paid subscription 'fee' of Kshs 40.00. He was jailed alongside with Herman Marine

Nderi, who was jailed for five years. He was also to become Nakuru Town Mayor after the second Multiparty General Election of 1997, under the auspices of Democratic Party (DP) of Kenya. The others were a Nakuru activist, Mwangi Mathenge Kaggia, four years, Francis Ndutha Karanja five years who also became councillors in Nakuru Municipality after 1992 General Election.

Kimunya, although working with the Nakuru Municipal Council, still actively engaged himself in politics. He told the late President Jomo Kenyatta, that *"If I leave active politics, I shall die very quickly"*. The late Kenyatta laughed at a rally and it is alleged that he allowed Kimunya to be in active politics, while he still worked at the Council until his retirement in 1986 as Deputy Housing and Estates Officer.

Kimunya, while in prison was transferred to Naivasha Main Prison, Kodiaga and Kiboswa Prisons and he completed his jail term at Kamiti Maximum Security prison, on August 4, 1989.

xv) **Salim Ndamwe:**

Ndamwe is among the founder members of the original Forum for Restoration of Democracy (FORD) together with the late Jaramogi Odinga and Lawyer James Aggrey Orengo among others. Ndamwe was arrested in 1989, arguably the first Pokot to fall out with the Moi government. He had a story to tell about his arrest.

"I was just a political activist. At that time, I was the Secretary-General of the National Development Party (NDP) that was formed before FORD. The party was formed by the late Oginga who was my friend.

"There was a government purge in West Pokot when I was arrested. The then District Commissioner (DC), Mr. Peter Lagat who was Moi's nephew led the purge. Any Pokot who was not singing the KANU tune was seen as a rebel. Other Pokots who were arrested along with me were Steven Krop Moroto, Micheal Lobuin, Namedo Toyoko and Ayub Kirui. The DC was the master-mind of our arrest."

188

He continued: *"The Special Branch police came to my home in Riruta Satellite at midnight. They told me that I was under arrest after conducting a search. They took me to Kilimani Police Station until the following day at about 10:00 a.m.*

"I was bundled into the back seat of a Toyota Saloon, sandwiched between two police officers and driven to the Traffic Police Headquarters.

"The man who appeared to me to be the team leader, at the Traffic Headquarters, approached me and said: 'In our mode of operations, we don't handcuff people. We only blindfold them and take them for interrogation and then set them free', he later told me that I will however, sit uncomfortably in their car. That meant in the boot of their car.

"Among the three men, who arrested me at my house, was one Petkay Miriti. He led officers to my house and carried me in a police vehicle to Nyayo House. Miriti warned me of an uncomfortable ride. When I came out of the boot of the car, I was already at Nyayo House. The car was parked next to the door of the basement into which I was frog-matched. We passed a small office, which I thought was a clerk's office, meant to keep the records of suspects booked at basement cells. Then we passed four doors leading to four cells. Mr. Miriti ordered me to choose one. I chose and when I entered it was locked. That was the last time I saw the man," he added.

(Miriti one time served as the Provincial Security Intelligence Officer (PSIO), Rift Valley Province, in the Moi-KANU regime. He was elected to parliament in December 2002 and appointed Assistant Minister for Trade and Industry.

Ndamwe described the cell at the basement as dark, painted red. At the time there was light from a bulb that was extremely shinny. It looked like a star.

"I stayed for about 41 days. Everyday I would be taken upstairs in a lift for interrogation. The officers would come, blindfold me and take me to the lift to the 24th floor. They

would order me to remove my clothes and remain naked and make me sit on the floor before the interrogators, numbering about 14. The group would question me for a long period as they at times would eat, drink and laugh at me.

"After lengthy questioning an officer waiting in the next room would be signalled and blindfold me then direct me to the lift down to cells to the basement. I wasn't physically tortured, maybe psychologically I was. When they came to my house and carried out a search, among the documents they carried with them was a letter from my doctor, Dr. David Ndetei, a Psychiatrist at Nairobi Hospital then. The impression was that I was mentally unstable, for I was under medication. I remember two times when I fell sick and was taken to Kenyatta National Hospital.

"During the time of interrogation my interrogators were asking me to be the principal government witness against some of the suspects. They (interrogators) wanted me to testify against one Mr. Cyrus Gitari Muraguri, who by then was also held at Nyayo House torture chambers. I accepted and was released and the other three were set free on the same promise of being witnesses.

"When we went to court to give evidence we all denied having been recruited to Mwakenya by Muraguri. It was before magistrate Onesmus Githinji and prosecutor Benard Chunga. We were all declared 'hostile witnesses' and Muraguri was set free as the case against him was dismissed.

"Prosecutor Chunga was very unhappy and shouted at the police for bringing 'useless witnesses'. The lawyer for Muraguri was Moses Wentangula.

"Message to Nyayo House Torture Squad: We shall forever remember what you did to innocent Kenyans, especially James Opiyo, Ismail Chelimo, Petkay Miriti, Peter Lagat and DC Kilonzo.

"A truth and reconciliation commission is the solution, which shall liberate you (torturers)."

CHAPTER TWELVE

Justice For Torture Victims: What Is Torture?

Definitions of torture vary slightly by different International Standards developed at different times. The UN Convention against Torture defines torture as any act which:

- Causes severe pain or suffering, whether physical or mental;
- Is intentionally inflicted on a person;
- For such purposes as obtaining from him or a third person information or a confession, punishing him for an act he or
- A third person has committed or is suspected of having committed or intimidating or coercing him or a third person, or for any reason based on decimation of any kind;
- When such pain or suffering is inflicted by or at the instigation of or with the consent or acquiescence of a public official or other person acting in an official capacity.

Torture is a serious crime against the person, like murder or grievous bodily harm. Torture has a further dimension – that of betrayal by the authorities responsible for protecting people from harm. Whether the perpetrator is a law enforcement official, or whether the institutions of the state have failed to provide protection from torture, the victims have been let down by the very people and institutions who have a legal duty to ensure their safety.

Crimes of Torture under International Law

Every act of torture is a crime under international law. Assistance and participation in torture are also crimes under international law.

- If torture is committed in an armed conflict, it constitutes the war crime of torture.

- If torture is committed as part of a systematic or a widespread pattern of similar acts, it constitutes the crime against humanity of torture.

- The UN Convention Against Torture prohibits torture as an independent crime, as a war crime and as a crime against humanity, absolutely and all circumstances.

- The Geneva Convention prohibits the war crime of torture in both international wars and internal conflicts such as civil wars or rebellions.

- The Rome Statute of the International Criminal Court prohibits torture when it constitutes genocide, a crime against humanity or a war crime.

- The prohibition of torture has a special status on international law. It is part of customary international law, which means it is binding on all states, whether or not they have ratified any of the international human rights treaties. It is also a "peremptory norm", which means that it cannot be overruled by any other law or by local custom.

The Moi Government's Justification for Torture

As contained in detention orders of July 1990, as against politicians: Kenneth Matiba and Charles Rubia

"You have been involved in subversive activities aimed at undermining and overthrowing the Government of Kenya as by Law established.

"You have associated yourself with and promoted the aims and objectives of an illegal and subversive body

under the name and style of Mwakenya whose purpose and objective is to overthrow the government of Kenya by unlawful means including use of violence.

"Pursuant to the said aims and objectives you have involved yourself in organizing and promoting an unlawful and illegal public meeting at Kamukunji Grounds, Nairobi, on July 7, 1990 whereas violence and other antigovernment activities would result.

"You have also aligned yourself to and associated with foreign elements including the press and other public media with the purpose of discrediting, maligning and scandalizing the government of Kenya and its constitutionally established leadership.

"You have further organized and recruited touts, matatu operators and musicians to record, produce and distribute seditious and subversive matter in the form of musical cassettes whose contents are calculated to incite and promote discontent, disaffection, ill-will and hostility among the people of Kenya.

"You have made utterances and conducted yourself in total disregard to the Head of State and have engaged yourself overtly or otherwise in antigovernment activities.

"Now therefore, because of these antigovernment activities and in the interest of preservation of public security your detention has become necessary."

As Against Journalists: Gitobu Imanyara

"You have been involved in subversive activities aimed at undermining and overthrowing the Government of Kenya as by Law established.

"You are the editor or proprietor or publisher of a Nairobi magazine known as The Nairobi Law Monthly in which, you have repeatedly written and published articles which denounce, ridicule and discredit the Government of Kenya, its activities and its established constitutional leadership. You've given lectures or speeches at Limuru Theological

College, on diverse occasions and on subjects which constitute or amount to downright subversion against the Government of Kenya as by Law established.

"You aligned yourself to and associated with well-known antigovernment characters and personalities such as Kenneth Matiba and Charles Rubia and others and have worked with them to lay groundwork for the formation of or creation of another political party contrary to the provisions of the Constitution of the country.

"You have participated with the same said characters in a series of illegal meetings in Nairobi and at these meetings, you and the said characters, have discussed and mapped out strategies to overthrow the Government of Kenya by unlawful means including use of violence.

"You have conducted yourself in total disregard to and disrespect of the Head of State and have participated in activities calculated to create disaffection, discontent, ill-will, hatred and hostility amongst the people of Kenya.

"Now therefore, because of these antigovernment activities and in interest of preservation of public security your detention has become necessary."

As Against Advocates: John Khaminwa and Mohamed Ibrahim

"You have been involved in subversive activities aimed at undermining and overthrowing the Government of Kenya as by Law established.

"You have associated yourself and established frequent contracts with well-known antigovernment characters and personalities like Kenneth Matiba and Charles Rubia.

"Under the disguise of legal consultations, you have indulged yourself in a series of unlawful and illegal meetings in Nairobi with the said antigovernment characters and, at those meetings, you and the said characters, have planned, discussed and mapped out strategies to overthrow the

Government of Kenya by unlawful means including use of violence.

"You have also, in conjunction with the same characters and others within the country conducted yourself and made utterances in a manner calculated to cause disturbance in the country, disaffection, dissatisfaction, discontent, ill-will and hostility among the people of Kenya.

"With the same said characters, you have discussed and promoted unlawful formation or creation of another political party in contravention of the provisions of the Constitution.

"You have made utterances and conducted yourself in total disregard and disrespect of the Head of State and have engaged yourself overtly or otherwise in activities aimed at creating alarm, despondency and fear among the people and inhabitants of Kenya.

"Now therefore, because of these antigovernment activities and in the interest preservation of public security your detention has become necessary."

.

EPILOGUE

Why Kenyans Had To Torture Fellow Kenyans
By Koigi wa Wamwere

"Torture is subjecting another being to cruel and inhuman conditions in order to force him or her to do or succumb to giving certain information or deliberately inflicting severe pain as a punishment in order to force an individual to say or do something. In Kenya, domestic violence is also torture. It is perpetrated to break spouse's resistance to domination. For example, the Moi-KANU regime was accused of torturing its political opponents or people with dissenting views.

"Most cases of torture are, however, perpetrated by government agents to force suspects to admit crime thus plead guilty.

"In police stations and remand prisons it is perpetrated to draw out confessions. In prisons it is used to stop criminals by destroying and killing them. In detention camps torture is used to break the will of political prisoners to resist dictatorship.

"Though Kenya is a signatory to the International Convention Against Torture, and Section 74 of the Constitution forbids torture, I don't remember a time when someone was charged with torture. The few times when police were charged with torture it was called assault to make the world over believe that Kenya's dictatorship perpetrated no inhuman treatment.

"Because the practice of torture was never acknowledged, forbidden or punished, in denial, it could only proliferate. The law did however permit one form of obvious torture that it never acknowledged as torture. Though legally and medically sanctioned and meted out by courts, prisons administering torture to prisoners with the express purpose of causing them injury, extreme pain that forces many to vomit and destroys their sexual potency.

"Aware of its extreme harm, this torture is administered only to men, the main enemies of the colonial authorities that introduced it and not to women. I heard of only one woman magistrate who advocated its administration to women prisoners in the name of gender equality. In Kenya, it is not just the Moi regime that has been guilty of torture. Kenya saw the worst torture during the Mau Mau war of national liberation. Colonial interrogators and screeners, beat, whipped, gave electric shocks, castrated, raped with broken bottles, African men and women whom they also crucified in the sun, tossed the victims into holes full of red ants and split them into two with two Land Rovers that tugged them in different directions.

"It is a shame that so far, neither Kenyatta nor Moi governments cared to investigate, condemn and demand reparations/torture that freedom fighters suffered in Manyani Government Prison or screening centres like Kwa Nyangweso at Bahati Nakuru District.

"At independence torture was not ended or its perpetrators punished. Kenyatta inherited both torture and its perpetrators whom he rewarded with power and positions of responsibility in the government.

"In the Kenyatta era, I saw police beat suspects brutally. I was however most horrified by the torture that JM Kariuki suffered before government agents assassinated him. The only comparable torture I heard of was that which the police under Moi perpetrated against Njenga Karanja of Nakuru.

"Though torture was perfected and made most routine in

the 1980s, the late Kenyatta and colonial torture should also be investigated and punished. Seeing colonial and KANU torturers in the past Narc government makes one wonder whether the post election violence Kibaki-Raila coalition is a sign of approval by the government or official disapproval of its condemnations by its victims and critics. In unearthing torture, investigations should not be limited to Nyayo House torture chambers under KANU; torture centres were many and scattered all over the country.

"Lake Nakuru National Park and detention camps in Manyani, Kamiti, Naivasha and Shimo La Tewa prisons were all torture centres. It is from this torture that Martin Shikuku, Charles Rubia, Kenneth Matiba and many others emerged from detention camps crippled and on crutches. All these centres of torture should be closed like the Robben Island Prison in South Africa and turned into museums and historical sites. Equally, torture teams were many and scattered all over the country. Only one team was in Nyayo House.

"Another notorious torture team was the Flying Squad of Inspector Kamunde that tortured and killed people from Nakuru to Makuyu. Justice Emmanuel Okubasu once called our prisons death camps. Before they became that, they were torture camps."

Why Did The Kenyatta Government Perpetrate Torture?

Essentially, it was to protect power by silencing dissidents. It was to break dissenters, critics, opponents, thinkers and even dreamers. But the purpose of torture went beyond this. Through destruction, it turned its victims into scarecrows. When masses saw them, they retreated into silence out of fear. Ultimately, through the persecution of individuals, the nation was itself tortured and silenced.

Democracies do not torture their dissenting citizens. Only dictatorships do. Just as opposition is a necessary consequence of dictatorship, torture to silence people is also a consequence of dictatorship. To the extent that Kenyatta's government was a dictatorship hostile to criticism and incapable of defending itself through argument, torture was inevitable.

Since it is impossible to extinguish people's desire for freedom and justice, in a dictatorship, the only way to avoid torture is for dictatorship to change.

In Kenya, the torture was like a scorpion. Its head was the President. It stung with the police to protect the head. In between the head and the tail, were prosecutors, judges and doctors.

The police did not torture people for and on their own behalf. Politicians ordered torture to protect their own power, wealth and persons.

They were its primary beneficiary. As leaders, it was their duty to protect innocent citizens against torture. When they failed to do so, they too committed torture. When people are accused of torture, our former presidents will be accused also. Without a dictator, there can be no torture.

Should compensation be paid to the victims of torture? While saying yes to this question, let me remind readers that no compensation can ever undo pain suffered, youth lost, years wasted, lives lost or hunger suffered by the family of the torture victims.

Notwithstanding, part of compensating victims of torture will be to relieve torturers of their power and responsibility in the government. How can a victim of torture trust the services or protection of a government whose ministers or police heads are former torturers? Only loss of power by torturers can make their victims feel safe.

In addition, not to repair ruined lives of torture victims is both an injustice and a perpetuation of torture. To feel sorry for victims of torture without giving them back their jobs is a waste of tears.

It is a mockery of justice, morality and humanity to

embrace the liberation that victims of torture suffered for and refuse to help them buy medicine to heal their physical and psychological wounds. People were not caught and tortured looking for treasure, gold and silver.

They were tortured fighting for liberation. If we like our freedom, we must be happy to compensate our soldiers who were hunted in the war of freedom. Only then can we ensure that others will arise and fight tomorrow if the need arises.

When Americans realized they were wrong to detain their Japanese citizens during the Second World War, they paid them compensation. When Germans admitted, they were wrong to torture and kill Jews; they too have been paying them compensation.

On behalf of the State, the government should not only pay victims, the British must also pay reparations for their torture of the Mau Mau.

Below is a view from local media:

"Many people reported receiving subversive literature anonymously and a 1987 statement purportedly from 'Mwakenya renounced KANU and the cynical philosophies of Harambee and Nyayoism'."

"The statement couched in classic Marxist phraseology said: 'The basic means of production, distribution and exchange are owned by imperialist foreigners and transnational corporations ... the ruling comprador class acts as an overseer; supervising the outflow of wealth into the Western Capitals'..."

Local Media House, 1987

Marine Nderi - former police officer jailed for 4
years, after jail became a mayor of Nakuru
town

Francis Karanja, jailed for 5 years, after sentence joined politics and was elected councillor
(FORD-Asili) now a political activist/farmer

DAILY NATION, FRIDAY, JANUARY 20, 1987

ATIONAL NEWS

Sedition: Kamangara and newsman jailed

By ANDREW KURIA

Kamangara: "Guilty"

Achira: "Apologetic"

DAILY NATION, January 29, 1987:
Kamangara (Late) and Achira after conviction and
sentence

CONCLUSION

In a book of this kind and size I cannot pretend to assert that I have comprehensively said everything about Mwakenya, December Twelve Movement or Pambana for that matter in Kenya during the Moi –KANU regime.

This book is merely intended to inspire other Nyayo House Torture victims and those who suffered in other detention camps in Kenya to document their experiences.

In that connection, I refer to the special report on 'The Mwakenya Files' – *Sunday Nation*, March 12, 2000 edition, pages 18 and 19, which was mainly attributed to dissident Kangethe Mungai.

The infamous Mwakenya trials raise eyebrows whenever they are mentioned at whichever quarters. It is worth noting that many of those who were victims (convicted and sentenced) of being members of the alleged clandestine organization were not necessarily so; some were not even aware of the so-called Mwakenya activities, if there were any.

In writing this book, I am expressing my beliefs and opinion, and cannot adequately speak on behalf of those who were arrested and arraigned in court, charged in relation to Mwakenya activities or programmes.

First, I dismiss with contempt the views of dissident Kangethe Mungai. To me, he is a person who was brought out by the then establishment to disorganize and water down the evidence against those who were allegedly involved in Mwakenya activities and programmes. Dissident Mungai's views were personal, self–defeating and portrayed him then as a person who was frustrated.

Equally, Mungai appears to have been bought out by the then Moi–KANU government to disorganize the evidence against those who were allegedly involved in arresting, intimidating, interrogating and conducting torture sessions at Nyayo House torture chambers against innocent Kenyan citizens; who were at that time expressing their views about the Moi–KANU government, which had gone astray in terms of management of the economy, education, health, while promoting corruption in almost all sectors.

Dissident Mungai, who may have been a member of Mwakenya, in his interview with writer Stephen Mburu of *Sunday Nation*, portrayed himself as a man who was in the inner circle or had been recruited by the then dreaded Special Branch officer, one James Opiyo who was in charge of those 'boys' who were based at Nyayo House Police Station torture chambers.

Most of the so-called Mwakenya convicts were actually critics of the Moi Government. The critics were generally branded as Mwakenya members to warrant the government agents to arrest them and instil total fear in the communities or institutions they (arrestees) came from.

I am at this point denying that there existed Mwakenya. If it was there, I did not know about it. The truth, however, was that many who suffered in the hands of Opiyo's dreaded Special Branch, were innocent. And this was the real reason why they were not allowed or given time to seek legal representation in court.

All those who appeared in court for stage–managed trials in connection with the then much talked Mwakenya, Pambana, and December Twelve Movement activities, were brought to court always after 5:00 p.m.! At the same time, there was an early arrangement before one was brought to court by the 'Opiyo boys' (read: interrogators) with the then Deputy Public Prosecutor (DPP) – one time Kenya's Chief Justice Benard Chunga and the late Chief Magistrate H.H. Buch. There were some Mwakenya suspects who appeared before either the late Joseph Mango or the Chief Magistrate Omondi Tunya.

For any right thinking Kenyan, or human being for that matter, if we were against corruption, mismanagement of public institutions, resources, the economy, deteriorating education, and poor health standards, it would defeat our purpose if we indulged in activities referred to by dissident Mungai as kill, maim, vandalize communication sector (telephones) acquire ammunitions, derail railway lines, among other things.

That, I was the only one from the larger Gusii community arrested, tortured and consigned to Kamiti Maximum Security Prison for two years! Now, the question is: Is it that I was conducting the so-referred to or called Mwakenya activities and programmes alone in the whole of Gusiiland?

The wonder of wonders was that I was not charged jointly with anybody or any group of people involved from the region!

This, in fact defeats justice. I therefore dismiss the entire exercise as stage–managed. My incarceration therefore, was meant to cow me from writing controversial reports and engaging myself in investigative journalism regarding the utilization and management of public resources of our country.

And how possible is what dissident Mungai is referring to; e.g. derailing the railway lines, destroying or vandalizing telephone lines, buying or acquiring of ammunitions and going to the bush/forest to wage underground war against the Moi-KANU government?

I recall well that President Moi's announcement on December 31, 1986, in Nakuru that there was clandestine organization called Mwakenya which was conducting oathing in the District and elsewhere (referring to the larger Nakuru District),

This triggered mass arrest of various people in Nakuru district and other parts of the country who were arraigned in court under the pretext of being Mwakenya members, oathing and conducting illegal activities meant to disorganize and de stabilize the then Moi-KANU government.

Among the first causalities, upon Moi's announcements included Francis Ndutha Karanja ('Mkombozi'), who later on became a Ford–Asili Councillor, Nakuru. Others were John Maina Kamangara, Joseph Karauri Miano (all deceased), Kimunya Kamana (former Nakuru Mayor) Herman Marine Nderi (also former Nakuru Mayor) and Kaggia Mathenge, just to list a few.

It is my sincere belief and conscience that there existed no Mwakenya, which was conducting oathing and illegal meetings to overthrow the Moi-KANU government. All was that during that time, if you were critical or against the establishment in the manner it conducted and managed the country's resources and its affairs in general, you were labelled as a Mwakenya.

Corruption and tribalism then (and today during Kibaki's reign) was very clear in government, parastatal appointments or employment sector for that matter. During the height or the peak of the so-called Mwakenya, anyone who questioned about the two factors (corruption and tribalism) in government, was obviously branded as a critic, dissident translated to mean Mwakenya and out to overthrow the government.

Therefore, the only remedy which was prescribed by the Moi-KANU government through its executioners, the then dreaded Special Branch, a unit of the Kenya police; was to crackdown those expressing dissenting views.

According to me and those whom we share similar sentiments, and were labelled as Mwakenya suffered untold and irreparable damages: our families, businesses, and professions were devastatingly affected in one way or the other.

All I wanted, and I believe those who were labelled as members of Mwakenya, was a country where justice reigned supreme as opposed to the unjust dictatorial regime of the then Moi-KANU establishment.

We (alleged Members of Mwakenya) wanted a Kenya which did not operate on tribal or ethnicity basis. All that you are seeing happening in this country today as wrongs and evils is what we were against and we expressed our sentiments and views openly whenever there was an opportunity and this is what was termed as Mwakenya activities and programmes!

The truth must be told and those Mwakenya victims must be compensated. Let's not distort history. Let's get the facts correct in regard to the then much publicized Mwakenya and other allegedly associated clandestine organizations.

"No amount of compensation would cover for mental, physical and psychological torture the Nyayo House victims went through. What we are asking for is just a token by the government as the sign of apology." - **The late Mirugi Kariuki, former Nakuru Town MP and Ex-detainee,** speaking in Parliament on April 9, 2003, while contributing to the motion on payment to torture victims.

Note: On July 21, 2010 Lady Justice Anne Okwengu awarded 21 Nyayo House torture victims a total of 39.2 million shillings.

AFTERWARD

By Gershom Otachi Bw'Omanwa

The story of Journalist Jimmy Achira is a reflection of experiences of many during the dark days of the Kenyan African National Union (KANU) under Daniel Arap Moi. It is important that the experiences such as Achira's be told for the sake of history and posterity. The history of those dark ages should be taught in our schools, alongside tales of heroic struggles such as that of Mau Mau.

Many Kenyans who now enjoy the fruits of "freedom" under multi-party democracy know little about the suffering many underwent and the sacrifices made to achieve the current political climate.

Indeed, for many in their twenties and thirties now, Jimmy Achira's story may read like a fairy tale as they grew up knowing Daniel Arap Moi as a comical and nice old man. Kenyans, in their otherwise admirable spirit of resilience and "moving on" with life and addressing the current "ills" (for instance "the fight against corruption" is now the fad), all too easily forget or gloss over serious historical human rights abuses.

The unspeakable repressive and torturous treatment of politicians like Jean Marie Seroney, Joseph Martin Shikuku and George Anyona by the regime of the late president Jomo Kenyatta was not simply copied but rather fine-tuned, Nyayo style, by Moi in his efforts to silence dissent and divergent beliefs and opinion. There are many examples of this including those of former cabinet ministers Kenneth Kenneth Matiba and Charles Rubia.

Others include lawyers John Khaminwa, Hon Gitobu

Imanyara, Hon James Aggrey Orengo and Hon Augustine Njeru Kathangu, among many others.

The current state of freedom of speech and press are often easily taken for granted. For almost three decades of independent Kenya, Voice of Kenya (VOK) (renamed the Kenya Broadcasting Corporation (KBC)) was the only bearer of "official truth". Divergent news or opinion by the press with any hint of criticism of powerful politicians was published at great risk to journalists and publishers. This was the case with *Society* news magazine- published and edited by Pius Nyamora (now in exile in the USA) in 1980s and 1990s.

I have known the author since my teen years. I have always known him as a brave and courageous journalist who speaks boldly his mind. For this courage he paid a heavy price. Whereas I had a general idea of the experiences he underwent in the hands of police and other state agents, the details in this book are more harrowing and sordid than I initially imagined. The book is a must-read for those keen on understanding the evolution of Kenyan politics and human rights. It would be useful especially for scholars and researchers that may wish to focus on when Moi took over after the late Kenyatta. The book is a modest and realistic presentation of what happened during the Moi-KANU regime which lasted for 24 years.

As a university student then, I witnessed the repressive acts of the state that led to disruption and (in some cases) total destruction of the careers of many student leaders who dared speak openly of societal injustices. Among the many cases are those of the Titus Adungosi (deceased), Paddy Onyango, Onyango Oloo, and Robert Wafula Buke, to name a few. As a young lawyer in the early 1990s I represented victims of state repression. One such case was the famous John Maina Kamangara (deceased) who, alongside twelve others was tried for close to eight years for committing the sin of attending a goat-eating function with friends.

Under Moi's rule all one had to do to destroy the career of a civil servant, a university student leader, a politician or any other person, was to arrange to "plant" a *Mwakenya, Pambana or December Twelve Movement* publications on him or her. The police (Special Branch or some other state agents) are largely suspected to have been behind such "planting" of what was termed "subversive literature" by the regime. They would then move swiftly to arrest the culprit. Once charged in court, the target became a pariah, shunned by even close friends and relatives.

Lawyers such as the Mirugi Kariuki (deceased), Rumba Kinuthia, Christopher Mulei (deceased) who dared challenge the unusual practices as night trials or who regularly represented such suspects often found themselves on the wrong side of the law. One always had to speak in hushed tones on the most basic of political issues in a restaurant, a pub or bar as the Special Branch (now re-branded National Security Intelligence Services - NSIS) and other state agents were all over the place. With their almost limitless finances and unfettered powers of police, prosecutor and judge rolled into one, they could arrest, interrogate, extract confessions through torture and detain a citizen for unlimited periods of time.

The author was a victim of such heinous practices. He speaks for many others that held divergent views at the time. My compliments and gratitude goes to the author for a job well done.

June 2010, Arusha- Tanzania

Bw'Omanwa is Defence Attorney at the International Criminal Tribunal for Rwanda (ICTR), Arusha Tanzania and Advocate of High Court of Kenya.

ABOUT THE AUTHOR

Jimmy Achira was born on May 20, 1956 at Bosiango Village of Bogichora Location, West Mugirango, Nyamira County, Western Kenya. He is the second born of the eleven children of the late Mzee Joseph Achira Mandere and late Mama Salome Nyanchoka Obanyi.

Achira went to Bosiango Primary School, in the then Nyamira District between January 1965 and 1971. After his Certificate of Primary Examination (C.P.E.) in 1971, he proceeded to Taranganya High School in Kuria and Nyansabakwa High School in Nyamira Districts respectively between 1972 and 1976.

After High School, he taught at Mborogo Secondary School in Nyamira District between 1977 and 1978, before venturing into journalism as his life long career.

In 1979–1980 he was a cub reporter with *Target/Lengo*, a fortnightly Christian-inclined newspaper, and 1980–1990 worked with the *East African Standard, Daily Nation and Sunday Nation, Kenya Times Group of Newspapers* as a Staff Correspondent both in Nairobi and Kisii, in Kenya, and Mwanza and Dar-es-Salaam in Tanzania.

During 1982–1986, he was a retained staff correspondent with *Nation Newspapers Ltd*. Between 1986 and 1990 he worked with *Daily News, Sunday News, African Business* and *New Africa*. He later worked for the *The Weekend Mail* and *The Weekly Review* as Assistant News Editor and Contributing Editor respectively in both

Kisumu and Nairobi. Away from the mainstream media, the author worked with the larger Catholic Diocese of Kisii's Planning, Administration and Development Offices as a Communications Coordinator and Editor of a Diocesan monthly Newsletter – *The Community*, between 1990 and 1992.

In April 1995, the author incorporated a publishing and a consultancy company – *Rural Media Services Limited* and started publishing a regional rural monthly newspaper – *The Western Monitor* of which he was the editor.

Journalist Achira, coedited one publication with Journalist Tom Amoro titled; *A Guide to Gusii Politics 1997*. He has also published another guide during the 2002 Transitional General Elections – *What Next After 1997 General Elections in Gusii?*

Presently, the author is the editor of *Electronic Forknews Journal*, published online under the umbrella of Electronic News Group (ENG Ltd).

Journalist Achira, received his Journalism training at one of the leading East Africa's oldest Journalism Schools (Nyegezi Social Training Institute (NSTI); School of Journalism Mwanza, Tanzania which later became a full-fledged University in August 1998 and was renamed St. Augustine University of Tanzania (SAUT).

The author later received further training at Thomson Foundation Institute (TFI), UK (1982). He is married to Lady Margaret Nyakerario Marucha and the couple is blessed with four children – Wycliffe, Douglas, Thomas and Mary Salome.

www.ingramcontent.com/pod-product-compliance
Lightning Source LLC
Chambersburg PA
CBHW020700270326
41928CB00005B/212